The First World War

an illustrated history by A. J. P. Taylor

A PERIGEE BOOK

TO JOAN LITTLEWOOD

A Perigee Book
Published by The Berkley Publishing Group
A division of Penguin Putnam Inc.
375 Hudson Street
New York, NY 10014

Penguin Books Ltd, Harmondsworth, Middlesex, England
Penguin Books Australia Ltd, Ringwood, Victoria, Australia

First published by Hamish Hamilton 1963; Published by Penguin Books 1966;
Reprinted 1967, 1970; Copyright © George Rainbird Ltd, 1963; Design by
Keith Burns

First Perigee edition: May 1972

ISBN: 0-399-50260-2

Cover by DON LONGABUCCO

The Penguin Putnam ⌐   Wide Web site address is
http://www.pe⌐   ⌐.com

Printed in the United States of America
         21   22   23   24   25

ACKNOWLEDGMENTS

The publishers express their thanks to the following who have supplied copyright illustrations for
this book:

The Imperial War Museum (Pls 13, 17, 20, 21, 22, 27, 28, 30, 38, 39, 40, 42, 47, 55, 58, 59, 64, 70, 71,
76, 77, 79, 86, 89, 98, 99, 102, 105, 106, 107, 115, 116, 134, 135, 137, 138, 144, 147, 160, 162, 165, 166,
168, 169, 175, 182); The British Museum (Pl. 56); The Radio Times Hulton Picture Library
(Frontispiece, Pls 7, 10, 14, 16, 32, 37, 40, 43, 50, 52, 53, 62, 75, 80, 82, 87, 92, 93, 96, 100, 103, 117,
118, 119, 121, 125, 126, 127, 129, 136, 142, 150, 152, 155, 158, 161, 163, 164, 167, 173, 176, 177, 178,
180, 186, 190, 191, 195, 198, 199, 200, 201, 203, 206, 214, 215, 220); The Gernsheim Collection (Pls 3,
113, 131, 156, 174, 187, 189, 202, 208, 211, 212, 216); Paul Popper (Pls 11, 12, 68, 114, 143, 205);
Camera Press (Pls 46, 97, 101, 104, 145, 146, 148, 159, 192, 193, 210, 213); P.A.-Reuter (Pls 4, 112);
Mirrorpic (Pls 63, 196, 221); Associated Newspapers (Pls 88, 130); Keystone Press Agency (Pl. 154);
Rex Features (Pl. 185); Fox Photos (Pls 217, 218); T. Jarvis (Pls 48, 60); Paul Tabori (Pls 29, 41,
44, 67); Dr Geoffrey Morey (Pl. 54); J. W. Dickenson (Pl. 72); Dr H. von Kotze (Pls 74, 84, 157);
Edmond Kapp (Pl. 132); C. A. Sinfield (Pl. 197); National Archives, Washington D.C. (Pl. 209);
Brown Brothers (Pls 15, 83, 85, 123); Bettmann Archive (Pls 69, 78, 109, 170); Culver Pictures (Pls
124, 181, 194); Gael Linn (Pls 110, 111); Bibliothèque Nationale (Pl. 207); Collection Viollet (Pls 9,
18, 51, 90, 91, 94); Jacques Boyer (Pl. 122); Museo Centrale del Risorgimento (Pls 65, 66); Bibliothek
für Zeitgeschichte (Pl. 26); Südd. Verlag Bild-Archiv (Pls 95, 179, 183); Ullstein Bilderdienst (Pls 5, 8,
19, 24, 25, 33, 45, 49, 57, 61, 73, 81, 108, 120, 133, 139, 140, 141, 149, 171, 172, 188, 204); Bildarchiv
d. Osterreicher Nationalbibliothek (Pls 1, 2); Hungarian News and Information Service (Pl. 219);
Tass News Agency (Pls 128, 151, 153); Bapty & Co. Photo Archives (Pls 5, 6, 23, 31, 34, 35)

Preface

The First World War cut deep into the consciousness of modern man. It reshaped the political order in Europe. Its memorials stand in every town and village. Half a century afterwards the experiences of it are not stilled. Each episode provides the subject for new books, many of them best sellers. My aim has been to see the war in historical perspective. I have tried to explain what the war was about; particularly, to resolve the paradox that men were passionately engaged in the war and hated it at the same time. Each country fought ostensibly to defend itself yet sought also to conquer and to make great gains. The statesmen were overwhelmed by the magnitude of events. The generals were overwhelmed also. Mass, they believed, was the secret of victory. The mass they evoked was beyond their control. All fumbled more or less helplessly. They were pilots without a chart, blown before the storm and not knowing where to seek harbour. The unknown soldier was the hero of the First World War. He has vanished, except as a cipher, from the written records. He lives again in the photographs.

War has always been the mother of invention. Historical photographs are among her children. Photography was raised from its infancy by the Crimean War. The pictures which Fenton took in the Crimea are the finest of his artistic creations. The Boer War was captured for posterity by the camera. These wars were far away. In the First World War, the camera could record the life of Everyman. It shows the statesmen and generals, on parade and off it. It shows the instruments of destruction. Photographs take us into the trenches and the munitions factories. We see again the devastated countryside and the queues for food. Here are the men who fought, suffered, and died; the human beings behind the ringing phrases. Thanks to the camera, we can relive the First World War, and not merely read about it. There were thousands of photographs from which to make a selection. We have thrown out ten for every one which we put in. Some, though well-known, imposed themselves. Many have not been used before. In the narrative, the war is an academic exercise, as remote from present experience as the great war of Troy. The illustrations show men. This war was our war too. Maybe, if we can understand it better, we can come nearer to being, what the men of that time were not, masters of our own destiny.

1. Their deaths started it all: Archduke Franz Ferdinand and his wife, with their children.

2. His last parade: Franz Ferdinand inspects troops at Mostar.

1914

On 28 June 1900 the Archduke Franz Ferdinand married Countess Sophie Chotek. It was a subdued, sad ceremony. The Archduke was heir to the Monarchy of the Habsburgs; he stood next in succession as Emperor of Austria, King of Hungary, and much beside. Sophie Chotek was a mere countess; she did not come within the permitted degrees for an imperial Habsburg marriage. Franz Ferdinand had to sign away the rights of any children born of the marriage. His wife did not become an archduchess or an imperial highness. Many devout monarchists felt that this augured ill for the Habsburg dynasty. None foresaw that Franz Ferdinand, on this wedding day, had fixed the date of his death, still less that this would lead to the deaths of many million others. For this wedding day ultimately set the fuse to the First World War.

Franz Ferdinand was a brutal and obstinate man, impatient with opposition, unsuited to a democratic age. He had one redeeming feature: he loved his wife. It irked him that she could never share his splendours, could never even sit by his side on any public occasion. There was one loophole. The Archduke was a field marshal and Inspector General of the Austro-Hungarian army. His wife could enjoy the recognition of his rank when he was acting in a military capacity. Hence he decided, in 1914, to inspect the army in Bosnia. There at its capital Sarajevo, the Archduke and his wife could ride in an open carriage side by side on 28 June – the anniversary of their wedding day. Thus, for love, did the Archduke go to his death.

Bosnia and its sister province, Hercegovina, were recent Habsburg acquisitions. Formerly Turkish and the scene of many rebellions, they had been administered by Austria-Hungary since 1878, annexed only in 1908. The inhabitants were southern Slavs, Serbs or Croats, many of them – especially the younger ones – resentful at having been brought under the Habsburgs instead of being allowed to join Serbia, their national state. Romantic young men conspired together, made attempts (unsuccessful) to assassinate Habsburg officials. When the Archduke's visit was announced, half a dozen grammar-school boys decided to have a shot at him. They received encouragement, and some crude weapons, from a Serb secret society. Its head, the mysterious Apis, was more concerned to embarrass his own government than to kill the Archduke. Apis made many plots. None of them came off until this one.

Even this success was chance. On 28 June the Archduke and his wife duly drove into Sarajevo. One young conspirator failed to draw his revolver; another felt sorry for the Archduke's wife and went home; a third threw his bomb, and missed. The Archduke reached the town hall. He was now angry: his wife's treat had been spoilt. He decided to drive straight out of town. But his chauffeur was not told. He took the wrong turning, then stopped the car and reversed. Gavrilo Princip, one of the schoolboys, saw before him, to his amazement, the stationary car. He stepped on to the running-board; killed the Archduke with one shot; aimed at an escort in the front seat and hit the Archduke's wife, sitting in the back, with a second. She, too, died almost immediately. Such was the assassination at Sarajevo.

It was more than a crime. It was a challenge to the position of Austria-Hungary as ruler of Bosnia; a challenge also to her prestige as a Great Power, which had been declining in recent years. Her statesmen were bound to demand some striking vindication. Why did this lead to a great war? Was some

3. He fired the first shot of the Great War: Gavrilo Princip arrested.

Power waiting only for an excuse, or perhaps had already decided to start a war in August 1914? Some historians think so. The Kiel canal, they say, was only widened for German dreadnoughts in July 1914; the German army was at the height of its superiority – in a few years the French and Russian armies would catch up with it. Other historians have discovered an unbearable tension in the relations of the Great Powers which was bound to snap. There was tension, of course, when five Great Powers faced each other in unbridled national sovereignty. This tension was no greater than in previous years, rather it was less. Germany and Great Britain were on more friendly terms, their naval rivalry dwarfed by agreement on the Bagdad railway and a future partition of the Portuguese colonies. France too, was moving towards friendship with Germany. In April 1914, a general election in France had returned a pacific majority of Radicals and Socialists. The German industrialists did not want war. They were convinced, with good reason, that Germany would soon become the leading Power in Europe from sheer economic strength. Again, many people in England and France were more apprehensive of Russia than of Germany. Good judges guessed that the future

4. Let cousinly love prevail: Kaiser William II instructs King George in horsemanship.

pattern would be an alliance of the three West European Powers – France, Germany, and Great Britain – against the Russian colossus. Everything was running in Germany's favour. Why spoil it by war?

Men are reluctant to believe that great events have small causes. Therefore, once the Great War started, they were convinced that it must be the outcome of profound forces. It is hard to discover these when we examine the details. Nowhere was there conscious determination to provoke a war. Statesmen miscalculated. They used the instruments of bluff and threat which had proved effective on previous occasions. This time things went wrong. The deterrent on which they relied failed to deter; the statesmen became the prisoners of their own weapons. The great armies, accumulated to provide security and preserve the peace, carried the nations to war by their own weight.

The rulers of Austria-Hungary had had trouble with Serbia before. This time they decided not to shrink. They turned for approval to their German ally. On 5 July they received it. William II, German Emperor, and Bethmann Hollweg, his Chancellor, told the Austrians to take a strong line; moreover, they promised German backing if Russia threatened to support Serbia. This was not a decision for war. Threats had brought prestige and peaceful success in the past; the German rulers assumed that the same would happen again. William II went off cruising in Norwegian waters; no one thought of warning Moltke, Chief of the German General Staff, who was also on holiday, that war might be round the corner.

The Austrians took their time. Always dilatory, they sought, in a leisurely way, some proof that the Serb Government had been involved in the plot at Sarajevo. They found no proof; none was ever found. However, on 23 July, the Austro-Hungarian Government sent an ultimatum to Serbia, with intent to humiliate her. On 25 July, the Serbs accepted with just enough reservations to save a scrap of prestige. Austria-Hungary at once broke off relations; the next day she declared war. This was far from a real war. It was a diplomatic manoeuvre, though a peculiarly violent one. The Austro-Hungarian army could not, in fact, be ready for many weeks.

Now it was Russia's turn. She was, or claimed to be, the patron and protector of the Slav states in the Balkans. She could not allow Serbia to be humiliated. Besides – a more practical consideration – if Germany and Austria-Hungary

dominated the Balkans, they would control Constantinople; their hands would be on Russia's jugular artery, the Straits, through which passed most of her trade with the outer world. Thus Russia's motive, too, was security, survival, not aggrandizement. The Russians wanted only to answer Austria-Hungary's violent diplomacy with some strong threat of their own – to mobilize, in fact, against Austria-Hungary as a diplomatic demonstration. Now intervened a vital factor of high strategy. All the European Powers had built up vast armies of conscripts. The plans for mobilizing these millions rested on railways; and railway timetables cannot be improvised. Once started, the wagons and carriages must roll remorselessly and inevitably forward to their predestined goal. Horses can be swapped crossing a stream; railway carriages cannot. The Austrians had already discovered that, if they mobilized against Serbia, they could not then mobilize against Russia; hence they had marked time. Now the Russians found that, if they mobilized against Austria-Hungary, they would be defenceless against Germany. General mobilization – not for war, but to keep their standing in the diplomatic conflict – was their only course. On 30 July they resolved upon it. The

5. Helmets and boaters: war is proclaimed in Berlin, 1 August 1914.

6. An Austrian army awfully arrayed . . .

Europe in 1914

Allied Powers
Central Powers
Neutral States

0   100   200   300   400   500
Miles

FINLAND

Petrograd

Moscow

R U S S I A

Minsk

Russian drive
on Tannenberg

Russian offensive in Galicia

Kiev

CASPIAN SEA

Odessa

CRIMEA

Sebastopol

Baku

RUMANIA

Bucharest

BLACK   SEA

BULGARIA

Constantinople

Angora

O T T O M A N

PERSIA

Athens

E M P I R E

Aleppo

Baghdad

CRETE

CYPRUS

Damascus

PERSIAN
GULF

SEA

Russians did not want a war, or plan one. They merely wanted to show that, when the Austrians threatened, they could threaten too. One bluff was piled on top of another.

Here the second factor of high strategy intervened to decisive and disastrous effect. All military authorities in Europe believed that attack was the only effective means of modern war, essential even for defence. They were quite wrong about this. They could have learnt from the Russo-Japanese War of 1904–5, and from the Balkan Wars of 1912–13 (or even from the American Civil War half a century earlier) that defence was getting stronger and attack more difficult. None of them learnt this. Every chief of staff had offensive plans, and only offensive plans. All hoped to win from the superior offensive spirit of their army. All except one. The German general staff did not believe that they could conquer decisively if they had to fight at full strength on two fronts, against both France and Russia at once. Therefore they had long planned, ever since 1892, to put practically all their armed weight in the west and to knock out France before the slow machine of Russian mobilization could lumber into action. It was often said in 1914, and has been often repeated since: 'mobilization means war'. This was not true. All the Powers except one could mobilize and could yet go on with diplomacy, keeping the armies within their frontiers. Mobilization was a threat of a high order, but still a threat. The Germans, however, had run mobilization and war into one. In this sense, Schlieffen, Chief of the German General Staff from 1892 to 1906, though dead, was the real maker of the First World War. 'Mobilization means war' was his idea. In 1914 his dead hand automatically pulled the trigger.

For the Russian decision to mobilize threw out the German timetable. If the Germans did nothing, they would lose the advantage of superior speed. They would have to face war on two fronts, not on one; and this, they imagined, they could not win. Either they had to stop Russia's mobilization at once by threat of war, or they had to start the war, also at once. On 31 July Bethmann asked Moltke: 'Is the Fatherland in danger?' Moltke answered: 'Yes'. This was the moment of decision. Germany sent an ultimatum, demanding Russian demobilization within twelve hours. The Russians refused. On 1 August Germany declared war on Russia; two days later, with hardly an attempt at excuse, on France. The First World War had begun – imposed on the statesmen of Europe by railway timetables. It was an unexpected climax to the railway age.

Schlieffen had not only laid down that the war must be won in the west. He had also directed how it was to be won. The short frontier between France and Germany was heavily fortified on both sides – no chance for a quick victory here. To the north of it lay Belgium, making a sort of funnel through which German armies could pass, then flood out beyond the French armies and encircle them. Schlieffen called this 'Cannae' – apparently forgetting that the victor of Cannae came ultimately to disaster. This was the Schlieffen plan – the only plan for war the Germans had. They put it into operation at once. On 2 August they demanded free passage through Belgium. The Belgians refused, and this refusal brought in Great Britain also. The British had hesitated until now, determined not to be drawn into what they called a 'Balkan quarrel', many of them reluctant to act even in support of France. The German demand on Belgium removed all doubts, except among a tiny minority. Great Britain entered the war a united nation. She was the only Allied Power to declare war on Germany, instead of the other way round.

Poor old Austria-Hungary took longest to get going. She had started all the upheaval, yet was the last to be involved. Prodded by the Germans, she declared war on Russia only on 6 August. Her troops crossed the Danube to invade Serbia on 11 August, and then to no good purpose. Within a couple of months they were thrown out, and the Serbs invaded southern Hungary. Great Britain and France were also tardy in breaking with Austria-Hungary; they declared war against her on 10 August. Another decision had been taken secretly. On 3 August, the Turks concluded an alliance with Germany, though hesitating to implement it.

All over Europe conscripts were joining their units. Troop trains were rolling to their allotted destinations. Crowds demonstrated enthusiastically in every capital, crying 'to Paris' or 'to Berlin'. The parliaments were equally unanimous, or nearly so. In England, on 6 August, a few members abstained from supporting the Government; none voted against it. In France Socialists became ministers for the first time, in the name of 'sacred union'. A minority of German Social Democrats opposed the war at the party meeting; they obeyed party discipline, however, and voted for the war in the Reichstag. William II was delighted with this behaviour of the Socialists, and exclaimed: 'I see no parties any more, only Germans.' The Austrian Parliament was not consulted. The Hungarian Parliament

7. The men of the mailed fist: William II, Supreme War Lord, with his generals.

was unanimously for war. Serb Socialists voted against the war, though their country had no choice; the Bolsheviks in the Russian Duma at first voted against the war also. These were disregarded voices. The peoples of Europe leapt eagerly into war. Yet for none of them was this a war of aggression. Every nation thought that it was defending its existence, though the method of defence was to invade someone else's territory. There had been no war between the Great Powers since 1871. No man in the prime of life knew what war was like. All imagined that it would be an affair of great marches and great battles, quickly decided. It would be over by Christmas. Men did not debate why they were fighting. They knew. It was to defend *la patrie*, the Fatherland, or Holy Russia. The British were in rather different case. Secure behind the guns of the Grand Fleet, they were in no danger of invasion. They had gone to war for a cause – the neutrality and independence of 'little Belgium'. Therefore the British talked, from the beginning, in idealistic terms. This was 'a war to end war'; 'to make the world safe for democracy'. The British would not be content with victory. They wanted somehow to make a better world. Later, their idealism was echoed in other countries. The British started it, and their disillusionment afterwards was therefore greater also.

Every Continental Power mobilized millions of men. In all, some six million went into the first battles – men doing their active service or recently sent to the reserve. Their commanders were elderly men who knew war only in the study or on manoeuvres. The supreme commanders – Joffre in France, Moltke in Germany, Conrad in Austria-Hungary, Grand Duke Nicholas in Russia – owed their position to favouritism or some twist of politics rather than to ability. The successful commander was the one who kept his nerve and refused to be shaken by the death and suffering inflicted on his orders. Few of the generals had heard a shot fired in anger; and they did not much increase their experience during the war – they remained far behind their armies at headquarters, drawing lines on maps, barking out orders over the telephone and surrounded by a sycophantic staff. The British generals had seen real fighting in the Boer War; that was a war of movement over vast spaces against an unseen enemy, a war of cavalry, and most British generals were cavalry men. Horses were everywhere. No army had any mechanical transport. There were a few motor-cars in

8. Heroes of the hour: German troops off to Paris, August 1914.

which generals and staff officers travelled when they con-
descended to get off their horses. The men slogged along on
foot once they reached railhead. Hence the extraordinary
contrast of the war: fast in delivering men to the battlefield;
slow when they got there. The armies could move no faster
than in Napoleon's time or in the time of the Romans when it
came to fighting. Indeed, they could not move as fast. For
reinforcements could always arrive by rail to a threatened
position before the attacking side could break through on foot.
Railway trains go faster than men walking. This is the strategical reason why the defence was stronger than the attack
throughout the First World War. Defence was mechanized;
attack was not. Supplies and guns were pulled along by horses.
In every army forage for the horses took up more space than
ammunition or food. Food supplies were essential. These mass
armies were too big to live off the country. They had to be fed
from their homeland. In this way the very size which had been
designed to bring victory made it impossible for the armies to
win or even to move.

There was a real war of movement only for the first month
or so before the initial impetus ran down; then followed four

9. French soldiers start their march from Paris to Berlin.

years of deadlock. Everyone expected the decisive campaign to be in the west; and they were right, though the decision was not what they expected. It was a decision against a quick victory, a decision that the war would go on indefinitely. The key to this campaign was the German advance through Belgium. The French had long known of this plan. They took no precautions against it. For one thing, they did not believe that the Germans could form divisions solely from reservists; hence they underrated German strength by nearly a third. In any case, they thought they had an answer. As the Germans struggled through Belgium, the French would strike their flank in the Ardennes and would also take a direct offensive in Lorraine; and, of course, according to official doctrine, the offensive always won. This offensive was duly launched on 14 August. It was a disaster. The French armies suffered here their heaviest casualties – worse even than the later casualties at Verdun. They lost the flower of their armies – the best officers, the most eager soldiers; a loss from which they never fully recovered. The French offensive shattered against the German fortifications; their soldiers, untrained for defence, fell back in confusion and disorder. Yet the defeat was a blessing

10. 'Now God be thanked who has matched us with His hour.'

11. Armies had to move at their pace.

in disguise; and the Germans erred in resisting the French attack so strongly. For Joffre, thanks to the failure of his offensive plans, had forces which he could move over to his left wing, and thus win the battle of the Marne – against all his expectations and maybe beyond his deserts.

The Germans had an easy time in their advance through Belgium. There was virtually nothing in their way; this is the only reason why, even at this early stage, the war of movement managed to move. Indeed Schlieffen's whole conception assumed the absence of any enemy – an astonishing assumption for a commander to make but, against all the rules, justified. The French were far away, getting themselves massacred against the fortified line in Lorraine. Only the small Belgian army opposed the Germans; and it soon drew back out of their line of march into the fortress of Antwerp. Liège had been expected to hold out for many weeks. Ludendorff, not yet a commanding general, took it by the simple expedient of driving through the main gate in a motor-car and demanding surrender. Then the citadel was battered to pieces by heavy Austrian howitzers. The Belgians pulled off one decisive stroke. They wrecked the railway lines. This cut down the flow of

12. Russian troops marching through Petrograd, no snow on their boots.

13. Belgian soldiers.

14. Belgian soldiers.

15. Their conquerors.

16. *Sir John French, commander of the B.E.F., in training for the retreat from Mons.*

German supplies and reinforcements. The German infantry of course made the whole advance on foot. This they did at a terrific rate: Kluck's First Army, which was on the outside of the circle, often covered thirty miles in a day. There was a price to pay. The German soldiers were tired men before they even sighted an enemy. The French tried to cut sideways into the German march, and advanced through the Ardennes. The Germans had foreseen this move, and thickened the side of their march as they went along. The French armies were shattered in their headlong offensive. Once stopped, they knew nothing of defence. The only alternative to advance was, they supposed, to retreat. They went reeling back in confusion and discouragement, defeated more by their own tactics than by the Germans.

The left wing of the French armies now hung in the air, bent back and petering out somewhere west of the Meuse. Further north in Belgium, the Germans were already getting beyond it. The French line received an unexpected extension. When the British entered the war, they imagined that they had a free hand to decide their strategy. Their expeditionary force, though small (not much over one hundred thousand men), could be sent anywhere thanks to the power of the British navy. On 5 August a Council of War met under Asquith, the Prime Minister; all the leading generals were present. They debated how to aid Belgium. Should the British force go to Antwerp? to Amiens? perhaps to Le Havre and then ramble over the countryside? or strike at Germany's heart by landing in Sleswig? Sir Henry Wilson, of the War Office, pulled the great men up short. Even the British Expeditionary Force, small as it was, could not move except to a prepared timetable; and only one had been prepared – a plan, drawn up in 1911, to place the B.E.F. on the French left. It was irrelevant to complain that this would not help Belgium – the ostensible reason why Great Britain went to war. It was this plan or nothing. The Council of War, and after it the Cabinet, reluctantly agreed. Thus British policy lost its freedom of action from the start. The B.E.F. was embedded in the Western Front, thanks to secret plans made by military technicians three years before the war started.

The British force was in position by 20 August, though far from knowing that the Germans were anywhere near. It fumbled forward, reached the mining town of Mons on 22 August. There the Germans blundered into it, equally surprised. On 23 August, two British divisions were attacked by two German army-corps; and held them off. The British rifle fire was so accurate – 'fifteen rounds rapid' per minute– that the Germans thought it came from machine guns. In fact the British had two machine guns for each battalion. The battle of Mons was a small affair by later standards, no bigger than some of the engagements in the Boer War. Still, it was the first British battle; and also the only one where supernatural intervention was observed, more or less reliably, on the British side. Indeed the 'angels of Mons' were the only recognition of the war vouchsafed by the Higher Powers. Sir John French, the British commander, was pleased with the battle. He intended to stand firm and fight again the next day. During the night he discovered his precarious position: the French army on his right falling back fast, and on his left no troops at all. The British army, too, had to retreat: falling back, day after day, an even harder feat of footslogging than that accomplished by the Germans. On 26 August the British had to stand and fight again at Le Cateau. Once more they held the Germans up and got away.

Then, a most extraordinary thing, no fighting followed for

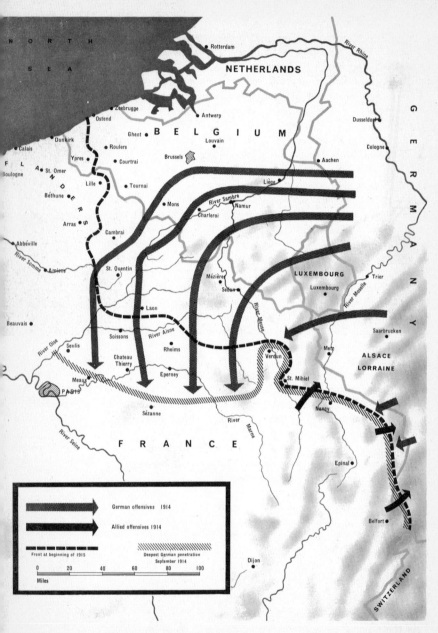

The German advance in the West.

nearly ten days. The B.E.F. was hanging on tight, as it were, to the French army on its right. The French were falling back due south; and the B.E.F. was pulled due south along with them, away from its lines of communications which ran to the west. The pull was so hard that soon the B.E.F. outdistanced the French in their rate of retreat. The Germans meanwhile had given a sort of backhanded flip with their left against the B.E.F. to knock it out of the way, and then resumed their march first due west, then inclining south-west. Thus the opposing forces were moving away from each other in their frantic marching. Sir John French even proposed to clear off altogether. Worried by the casualties in his small army – trivial though these were by later standards – he announced his intention of withdrawing to St Nazaire, on the Atlantic seaboard of France, in order to refit. He changed his mind only when Kitchener, now Secretary of State for War, crossed to Paris in field marshal's uniform, and ordered him to stay in line. The French Government and Parliament fled from Paris to Bordeaux. Paris was now in 'the zone of the armies'.

As the Germans swung round into France, there appeared the great, the insuperable, flaw in Schlieffen's plan. This flaw

17. The plane which detected von Kluck's swing away from Paris.

18. General Gallieni who, according to Joffre, did not win the battle of the Marne.

was Paris. If Kluck's army on the extreme German right went west of Paris, there would be a great gap between it and Bülow's army which came next in line; if Kluck went east of Paris, he could be attacked on the flank. Schlieffen had foreseen this flaw, and had failed to suggest means of overcoming it. The Germans could not pump in new forces with which to 'contain' Paris; their lines of communication were already crammed. Kluck's advance wavered to and fro like the tentacles of an octopus. Then he decided to go east of Paris in the hope of encircling the French armies before the Paris garrison broke out. Moltke, from his distant headquarters, approved this decision.

Meanwhile, the French were trying to restore their shattered position. Joffre showed admirable calm in adversity, never missing his two well-cooked meals a day. He dismissed subordinate generals right and left. His only strategical idea was to retreat, keeping a straight line, and to push forces over to his left; then at some point, he would hit back at the Germans head-on. Gallieni, the military governor of Paris, had a different idea. He saw things from the angle of Paris; and therefore saw the exposed German flank. Far from wanting to stop the German advance, as Joffre did, he wanted to let it go on and then catch

The battle of the Marne.

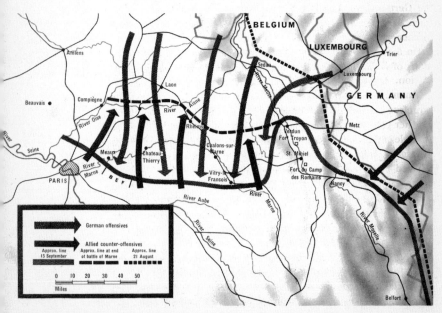

the Germans in the rear. When Joffre moved forces towards Paris in order to lengthen his line, Gallieni sent some of them further north to get behind the Germans.

On 5 September the Germans crossed the Marne. Then the plans of Gallieni and of Joffre exploded. They were in contradiction. Gallieni was hoping to close the sack behind the Germans. Joffre was hitting at the bottom of the sack, and therefore actually driving the Germans out of Gallieni's trap. Neither plan worked out. Kluck had been going full tilt east to encircle the French when he learnt of Gallieni's preparations on his right flank. He turned west again. Gallieni had been kept starved of men, and could not make headway against Kluck north-east of Paris. Further east, Bülow's army held firm against Joffre's direct offensive. But an enormous gap opened between the armies of Kluck and Bülow. Sir John French was at last persuaded by Joffre to stop his retreat. When the British advanced, they found no enemy: only a hole. On each flank of them, the French were fighting fiercely. The British went forward into emptiness. There were virtually no British casualties on the Marne. The British did not realize their advantage. They moved forward anxiously, almost timidly.

19. Moltke asked: 'Where are the captured guns?' Some were being paraded through Berlin, September 1914.

After their terrible experiences previously they could not believe what was happening, that there was no enemy facing them. The B.E.F. only covered eight miles a day, instead of the thirty miles a day which it had kept up during the retreat. Of course the men were tired; but the real failure was in leadership, which was blind and unenterprising. Even so, the British cavalry were sometimes forty miles behind the enemy lines.

Moltke, far away, was worried. He had never felt much confidence in the campaign. He kept asking: 'Where are the prisoners? Where are the captured guns?' There were few. Wireless was crude in those days; the field telephone worked badly over two hundred miles of cable. On 8 September, Moltke sent a staff-officer, Major Hentsch, to find out what was happening. Hentsch found Bülow anxious about his exposed right, and on the point of retreat. The next day, he found Kluck holding his own against the French troops from Paris, but unable to protect his rear. Hentsch authorized a general retreat. Everywhere the Germans began to roll back. High Allied officers talked of being in Germany within a month, or even three weeks. The Allied advance, in fact, lasted five days. On 14 September the Germans reached the Aisne. They were exhausted, could march no more; they were joined by some fresh troops, released by the fall of Maubeuge. The Germans scratched holes in the ground, set up machine guns. To everyone's amazement, the advancing Allies hesitated, stopped. The campaign was over. One man with a machine gun, protected by mounds of earth, was more powerful than advancing masses. Trench warfare had begun. The war of movement ended when men dug themselves in. They could be dislodged only by massive bombardment and the accumulation of reserves – warnings which always gave the other side time to bring up reinforcements. The machine gun completed the contrast between the speed with which men could arrive at the battlefield by rail, and the slowness with which they moved once they were there. Indeed they did not move at all. The opposing lines congealed, grew solid. The generals on both sides stared at these lines impotently and without understanding. They went on staring for nearly four years.

The battle of the Marne had a sequel, a last splutter of the war of movement. Both lines still hung in the air, petering out north of the Aisne. Both sides tried to turn the flank, to get ahead of the other. This was called 'the race to the sea', though it was an open flank, not the sea, which they were racing for;

and arrival at the sea meant that they had failed. The Germans
grasped the idea first, while Joffre was still dreaming of a
further head-on advance. On 14 September – the very day when
the lines first stuck – William II dismissed Moltke, and put
Falkenhayn, Minister of War and a better general, in his place.
Falkenhayn at once began to prepare a more modest Schlieffen
plan of his own. But the Germans were running short of armies.
Their only available forces were tied down before Antwerp,
besieging the Belgian army. Joffre, as usual, missed the
importance of this. He despised the Belgians and refused to
send them any assistance. Kitchener in England took the same
attitude. Winston Churchill, not content with running the
Admiralty, rushed in to fill the gap. He sent 3,000 marines to
Antwerp, with himself as prospective commander. Such aid
was not enough. Antwerp fell on 10 October. Most of the
marines were interned in Holland. Even so, the defence of
Antwerp achieved great things. It distracted the Germans from
'the race to the sea' while their way was still open. By now,
even Joffre was moving forces north. The Belgian army,
escaping from Antwerp, held the Germans on the coast itself, *20. German*
largely by opening the sluicegates and flooding the country. *soldiers manufac-*
The German advance was pushed inland. *turing electricity*
by bicycle.

21. *Germans digging their first trenches.*

In mid-October the Germans moved towards Ypres, meaning to outflank the enemy, at exactly the moment when the British, moving up from the Aisne, arrived at Ypres with the intention of outflanking the Germans. The two offensive plans ran into each other quite accidentally. The Germans were the stronger. The British were not only weaker in numbers, but badly led, with Sir John French bouncing from extremes of confidence to gloom. At one point the Germans punched a hole right through the British lines: ahead of them were only cooks and batmen. As always happened, the defence brought in new men by rail faster than the attackers could move forward on foot. Once more the line thickened and settled down. This mutual battering, though called the first battle of Ypres, was far removed from warfare of the old style. Men were fed in day after day on a narrow fortified front; there was much slaughter and no result. The B.E.F. suffered heavier casualties at Ypres than throughout the previous campaign. The British regular army was shattered, leaving only a framework for the new mass armies that were to come.

The Western Front was now drawn from Switzerland to the sea. Expectations of a short decisive war had proved false. But

22. Problems of horse transport for the B.E.F.

this first rushing campaign left its mark. Though the Germans failed to encircle the French armies, they were left with nearly all Belgium and with the industrial region of France. The French had lost most of their coal supplies, all their iron fields, and much of their heavy industry. Joffre, strangely, came out with enhanced reputation which kept him in supreme command for two more years. Yet the surprising thing in retrospect is that the Germans were allowed to succeed at all. They had been moving round the outside of a circle on foot, while the French could send troops straight across the circle by train. They sent them belatedly because Joffre did not grasp his strategical opportunity. The man who lost north-eastern France by his obstinacy became in 1916 the first marshal created in France since the fall of Napoleon III. Such are the quirks of war.

There had been great engagements, and great disappointments, on the Eastern Front also. Here the Russian steamroller had been expected to carry all before it. In reality the Russians had made little preparation to invade Germany. They botched something up to aid their western allies. Two Russian armies pushed at random into East Prussia, where there were few German troops. Prittwitz, their commander, took fright and proposed to retreat behind the Vistula. Moltke dismissed him abruptly, and sent over Ludendorff, supposedly the coming man on the German staff. Ludendorff was not of high enough rank to hold supreme command. An elderly general, Hindenburg, was dug out of retirement to act as cover for him. The two men met for the first time on Hanover station, Hindenburg buttoning himself into an old uniform that was now too tight. When the new commanders arrived in East Prussia, they found that Hoffmann, of Prittwitz's staff, had already put things right. He had made the most of the wide gap between the two Russian armies, separated as they were by the Masurian Lakes; he had also benefited from the casual Russian habit of sending their wireless messages en clair – code was too difficult for them. Hoffmann pulled the German troops back from the north where they were opposing one Russian army; but, instead of retreating, moved them further south, where they encircled and destroyed the second. 90,000 Russian prisoners were taken. One Russian army was broken; the other fell back in disorder. This was the battle of Tannenberg (29 August). It cleared German territory for the duration of the war.

Further south in Galicia, vast forces of Russians and

23. German harbour police search a Belgian dockyard worker.

24. Victims of war: homeless Germans in East Prussia.

25. *The trail of war: market place at Ortelsburg after the battle of Tannenberg.*

Austrians were locked in confused conflict. The railway network of western Europe virtually gave out here. Instead there were great empty spaces where armies, ill-equipped by Western standards, wandered in search of each other; straddled across each other's lines of communications; encircled the enemy and were in turn encircled to the bewilderment of their respective headquarters. Both armies suffered heavy casualties, and were threatened by disaster. In the end, the Russians came out victorious from sheer weight of numbers. By the close of October, the Austrians had lost Galicia; Russian troops reached the Carpathians. They were soon checked by the arrival of a German general and German troops. In the east, too, a front line was drawn. It was never so solid as in the west. The trenches were lightly held. Cows grazed and peasants tilled the soil between the two lines of trenches. An attacking force could advance fifty miles or so if carefully reinforced. Then the impetus of advance gave out, through lack of railways. The defenders, falling back on their supplies, consolidated their position; the line formed anew. This persistence of the Eastern Front was a great misfortune for the Germans. Though their territory was not threatened by invasion, they had to maintain a strong force in the east to stiffen the crumbling

26. The supreme war lords: Hindenburg and Ludendorff.

Austro-Hungarian army. Their worst fear was fulfilled: they had to fight a 'war on two fronts'. Yet they achieved what had been dismissed as impossible before the war; they held both these fronts securely so long as they stood on the defensive, and had forces to spare for other fronts besides. The Schlieffen plan had been unnecessary after all.

Thus, on land there were great battles both west and east, but no decision, only deadlock. At sea there was also deadlock, though no battles; this was itself a decision. The Germans had been preparing for years a battle fleet with which to challenge British maritime supremacy. When war came, they failed to do so. The German High Seas Fleet remained obstinately in harbour. The 'Armageddon', so constantly prophesied for September 1914 by Admiral 'Jacky' Fisher, did not take place. Moreover the Germans, in their obsession with battle-ships which they then failed to use, had neglected to build ocean-going commerce-raiders. Two of their cruisers, the *Goeben* and the *Breslau*, were in the Mediterranean when war broke out; they managed to escape to Constantinople, and their guns forced Turkey into the war at the end of October. Another cruiser, the *Emden*, ravaged British shipping in the

Indian Ocean. Seventy-eight British ships hunted her, before she was caught and destroyed by the Australian cruiser *Sydney*. The only sizeable German force at large was a squadron under von Spee, which started from Chinese waters and then crossed the Pacific. It ran into an inferior British force under Cradock off Coronel on 1 November, and sank his two cruisers virtually without German casualties. Churchill and Fisher, now restored as First Sea Lord, at once sent two battle cruisers to the South Atlantic. Von Spee was tempted to destroy the British wireless station on the Falkland Islands, where – unknown to him – the British battle cruisers happened to be coaling. On 8 December it was his turn to be outgunned. Four out of his five ships were sunk, this time with few British casualties. The fifth escaped, only to be sunk the following March. From then on, Britannia ruled the ocean waves so far as surface ships were concerned.

The pre-war naval planners had thought only of big ships with big guns. Both sides failed to foresee the importance of new weapons, mines and submarines, though the Germans were slightly better equipped than the British. These, not battleships, were the cause of British losses: *Aboukir*, *Hogue*, and *Cressy* were all sunk by a single U-boat on 22 September;

27. *Austrian cavalry searching in vain for the enemy.*

the battleship *Audacious* was sunk by a mine on 27 October. The Admiralty were so perturbed by this latter loss that they kept it secret until the end of the war. Moreover, the British had carried their neglect of these new weapons so far that they had not protected Scapa Flow, the base of the Grand Fleet, from submarines. In November the alarm (false in fact) of an enemy periscope sent the British navy in flight first to the west of Scotland, then west of Ireland. It did not return to the North Sea until well on in 1915. The Germans seized the opening to bombard the British coast twice. They killed a number of people; broke the windows of many boarding-houses at Scarborough; damaged Whitby Abbey. On a third raid, they were caught by British battle cruisers and badly knocked about. The Germans did not come out again for a long time. The British Isles were safe from invasion. Of course, equally the British could not land in Sleswig; but then, as Bismarck once said, they would have been arrested by the police if they had. This was a trivial matter in comparison with the great British achievement: the enemy fleet had been routed, though without a battle. Few appreciated at the end of 1914 that the struggle against the new weapons at sea was still to come.

The wide oceans were open to British shipping. Supplies of food and raw materials could come in as securely as in peacetime, until the German submarines started to operate. British credit seemed inexhaustible. The British, too, stumbled on a new weapon, less dramatic than the U-boat but even more effective: they gradually cut off German supplies. They could no longer operate the close blockade of previous wars. Mines and submarines made it impossible for British warships to cruise off the enemy ports. Instead the British built up a system of invisible blockade, imposed from a distance. German ships were arrested; neutral ships brought into a British port, and their cargoes checked. Then, to make things easier, British consuls in far-away ports issued neutrals with a clean bill. It took some time to get things going. The neutrals resented being rationed in their essential supplies. The Americans protested against interference with their trade, and defended the principle of 'the freedom of the seas'. On the other side, the Germans had been without foresight. They had failed to stock up with the raw materials of war. They imagined they would still be able to buy in the world markets. Moltke even refrained from invading Holland so as to keep open a channel for German commerce with the outer world. The noose round Germany's

neck tightened very slowly, but it was in the end a powerful element in her defeat.

The war, though dignified later with the name of the First World War, was largely confined to Europe so far as large-scale combat was concerned. But men from the rest of the world were drawn in; and fighting, though less intense, ranged wide. The British Dominions were technically committed by the declaration of war for what was still legally a united Empire; all made great voluntary efforts to the common cause. Canada sent an army to France; Australia and New Zealand contributed at once to the garrison of Egypt. Indian troops were used in France, where the climate hampered them. They were also sent to secure British oil supplies in the Persian Gulf, and there were gradually involved in the conquest of Mesopotamia— a meaningless and disastrous campaign. The South Africans conquered German South-West Africa, after first overcoming a rebellion of Boers who had not forgotten or forgiven the Boer War. Most of Germany's other colonies in Africa were easily overrun – more to have something to bargain with if it came to peace negotiations than for their value, or perhaps merely because it was a British tradition to make colonial gains in wartime. The

28. The ship which brought Turkey into the war: the Goeben *is repaired after striking a mine.*

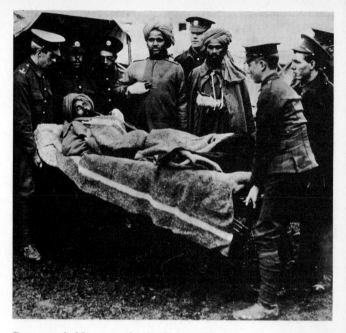

Germans held out only in East Africa – a romantic and troublesome affair which went on until after the armistice of November 1918. In the remote Far East Japan loyally entered the war as Great Britain's ally and also to her own great profit. She carried off Germany's sphere of Shantung, and then went on to turn the whole of China into a sphere of her own – the beginning of a development which was ultimately to bring Japan great victories and then calamitous defeat in the Second World War.

One Great Power remained virtuously aloof. Though a few Americans sympathized warmly with the Allied cause, most were firm for neutrality. The ancestors of these Americans had, after all, left Europe so as not to be involved in European affairs; they saw no reason to go back now. Many were of German stock. The Irish in America, unaffected by the wave of enthusiasm for the war which was sweeping Ireland, were vocal against supporting the British oppressor of their old country. President Wilson, from the first, cast himself in the role of peacemaker. Not merely could a neutral mediate between the warring states. She could, Wilson thought, impose generous terms upon them when they were sufficiently exhausted; terms which would ensure a lasting peace and which the undiminished strength of the United States would guarantee. Meanwhile the Americans combined virtue and profit. They grew rich, supplying Allied needs; at the same time, they had a firm conviction that they were following the best course for the future of the world in the long run.

As 1914 drew to its close, the pattern had been drawn for the First World War, a pattern not foreseen by anyone in a responsible position before the war started: not a short war of quick decisions, but a war of deadlock and prolonged battering which seemed as if it might go on indefinitely. No one had prepared for this; no one knew how to handle it. Millions of men had been mobilized in every Continental country without any realization that they would be away for years. Now the whole of civilian life had to be adapted to their absence; and millions more men had to be provided to replace those who fell. At first older men could be called up; and the mass armies saw a further great expansion until about 1916. Then the armies had to wait for the annual class – the youngsters who were reaching military age. This was a severe handicap for the French, whose birthrate had been progressively 'declining; it

30. Civilization comes to Africa: burning a native village in the Cameroons.

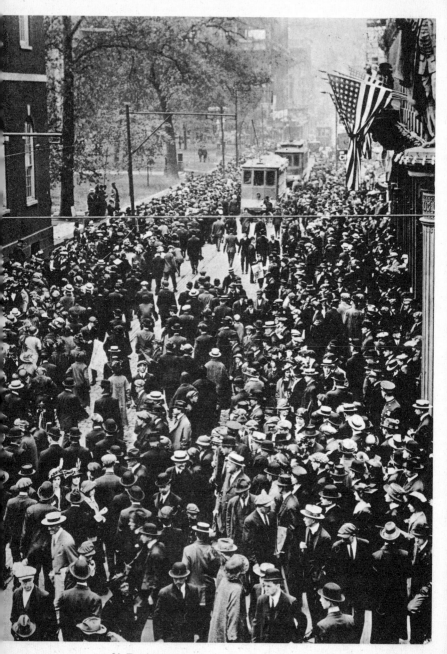

31. Patriotism at work: German Americans demonstrate for neutrality.

32. Scraping the barrel: French boys of 18 join the army.

was an advantage for the Germans whose birthrate kept up until the beginning of the twentieth century – and the Germans actually increased their armies until the spring of 1918, despite much talk of 'attrition' on the Allied side. Russia of course had always unlimited manpower. Her trouble was that she had little to equip them with. As early as December 1914 Grand Duke Nicholas, the Russian commander, warned his allies that the Russian armies were incapable of further offensive action. Shortage of material did not hit only Russia; all the belligerents were affected by it. Here too, plans had been laid only for a short war: the armies, it was assumed, would win (or lose) with the equipment which they possessed at the beginning. Now not only had the armies to be equipped anew, but far more had to be provided. The armies were bigger than had been expected, and their needs greater. The First World War was, in some ways, much greedier of munitions than the Second – not in machines, tanks, and aeroplanes, but in guns and shells. The barrage, growing ever heavier and more prolonged, became the outstanding feature of the First World War. Factories sprang up all over Europe solely to feed it.

This demanded little short of an industrial revolution. New

industries, and with them a new economic system, had to be created almost overnight. Workers were persuaded, or compelled, to change their jobs and to relax their peacetime standards. Employers worked to government order. The French did best with this; they had a tradition of economy planned for war which went back to Napoleon. The Germans took longer to get going, but then acted to greater effect. The inspiration for the new system came largely from Walter Rathenau, a great capitalist of Jewish origin; without him, Germany could hardly have carried on the war at all. The war brought also new social problems: problems of welfare for the soldiers and munition workers; problems of maintaining the wives and families of the absent soldiers; above all the terrible problem of 'profiteering'. Inevitably, huge profits were made in the helter-skelter of wartime production and rising prices; inevitably also, this caused a rising discontent, which in the end reached the point of revolution in many European countries. The profiteer, in his top hat, drinking champagne while men died, became the dominant symbol in revolutionary propaganda. Little was done to stave him off. None of the belligerents tried to pay for the war out of taxation. Some, including

33. Rathenau: the man who organized Germany's economy for war.

34. Manifestations of war in all their artistry.

Germany, even reduced taxes in order to alleviate the hardships of war. Ultimately, it was assumed, the enemy would pay. Meanwhile there were appeals for patriotic War Loans. In Germany anyone subscribing to these loans could hammer a nail into a huge wooden statue of Hindenburg.

The Continental countries had all been militarized before the war; they only needed now to push further along the same course. The British people faced much greater changes. They lived in a free trade, free enterprise country. The 'State' hardly existed except to maintain order. There was no compulsory military service, and no experience of foreign wars. The regular forces were expected to do the fighting. The navy would guard the seas; the expeditionary force would slip over to France, engage the enemy, and then come back again. Winston Churchill announced the slogan: 'Business as Usual' – the notice which a shopkeeper stuck up when his stock had been damaged by fire. All this was changed by the inspiration of a single man, Kitchener. He was generally regarded as the greatest British soldier still in active life: conqueror of the Sudan and of South Africa, Commander-in-Chief in India, now ruler of Egypt. Though he had been out of the country for

36. The Profiteer's Flag.

forty years, he happened to be in England when war broke out, and was hastily made Secretary of State for War in order to sustain the somewhat shaky prestige of the Liberal Government. He startled his new colleagues at the first Cabinet meeting which he attended by announcing that the war would last for three or four years, and that Great Britain would have to raise an army of many million men. This forecast was not based on any profound knowledge: the entire general staff, which was supposed to do the strategic thinking for the British Empire, had gone off to France with the expeditionary force. Kitchener operated by flashes of inspiration. Lloyd George compared his mind to a lighthouse, which sent out a penetrating beam for a moment and then left utter darkness, as the light revolved.

The British Cabinet were against conscription. Kitchener had to rely on voluntary recruiting. The machinery for this already existed in the shape of the Territorial Army, now eleven divisions strong. Kitchener despised these 'week-end' soldiers, and set out to raise a new regular force, Kitchener's army. His picture glared balefully from every hoarding in the country, forefinger outstretched: 'Your Country needs YOU'. Kitchener had expected to get perhaps one hundred thousand volunteers in the first six months, and maybe five hundred thousand altogether. This was all, and more than all, that the existing factories could equip with rifles and uniforms. These modest plans were submerged by a wave of patriotic enthusiasm. Five hundred thousand volunteered in the first month; and the recruitment rate ran at over one hundred thousand a month for eighteen months thereafter. Altogether, Great Britain raised more than three million volunteers. This mass army was not produced by design; it was thrust on a Government and a War Office which did not know what to do

37. Horatio Bottomley, the People's Tribune, earns his keep.

with it. The method was clumsy. The best men volunteered first, and usually those who could least be spared. The civilian departments made desperate, largely unsuccessful, efforts later to recover coalminers and skilled engineers from the fighting line. The army was not prepared to receive so many men. There were few camps, and little equipment. All through the winter of 1914–15, men lived under canvas, and drilled in civilian clothes, with walking-sticks instead of rifles, when they had expected to fling themselves at once on the enemy. It was the beginning of their disenchantment.

Voluntary recruitment had another consequence: enthusiasm had to be maintained and whipped up. Leading politicians stumped the country, winning popularity for themselves and implanting the passions of war in their audiences. Lloyd George acquired here a new fame. He had opposed entry into the war until the last moment. When the war came, he agreed to handle the financial problems, without committing himself to approval of policy. Suddenly, on 19 September, he appeared on the public platform, as fervent a supporter of the war as though he had backed it from the first. Lloyd George had the demagogue's touch. Most politicians could not shake off their parliamentary training, and spoke in ponderous, measured tones. They were eclipsed by Horatio Bottomley, a discredited bankrupt before the war, now fully restored as the People's Tribune. Bottomley was the most successful of recruiting orators. His peroration varied with the size of the 'take' – simple patriotism for less than £100; bringing in Jesus Christ, the Prince of Peace, at more than that; leading his audience to the foot of the Cross when they had paid more than £200. Bottomley pulled in many recruits; he also pulled in £78,000 for himself, money at once squandered on racehorses, women, and champagne.

By such means, public feeling in England was brought to white heat. It was hardly cooler in France and Germany. Everywhere men were stirred by righteous passion, and thrust eagerly forward for sacrifice. Rupert Brooke spoke for an entire generation: 'Now God be thanked who has matched us with His hour.' He died soon afterwards, from the bite of a mosquito. Ignorance inflamed passion further. Men crowded to buy special editions of the newspapers, but the newspapers contained no news. The generals did not want to be embarrassed by civilians looking over their shoulders. There was a rigorous censorship which forbade all military news. War correspondents were not allowed anywhere near the front. The British people

were not told that the expeditionary force was retreating from
Mons; the French were not told that their armies had lost the
battle of the frontiers; the Germans were not told that the
Schlieffen plan had failed to win the war. The facts, when they
gradually came out, only inspired men to further frenzy.
Where hard news was lacking, rumour flourished. A hundred
thousand (or according to other accounts a million) Russian
troops were reported to have landed at Aberdeen, and passed
through England on their way to the Western Front. Everyone
knew some other person who had seen them; many claimed even
to have seen the snow on their boots. A mountain of myth grew
over the atrocities which the Germans were supposed to have
committed in Belgium. Babies had their hands, nuns their
breasts, cut off. An innocent story that church bells were rung
in a Belgian village, to warn of the coming of the Germans,
became, when passed from hand to hand, the solemn assertion
that the Germans had tied the village priest to his bell and
used him as a live clapper. Some of these stories were fabri-
cated by ingenious journalists for want of better material;
most sprang from the general conviction that war was like
that.

In no country could men believe that they were being beaten by mistake. Hence they looked round for spies or for traitors in high places. German soldiers were said to operate disguised as nuns, and could be detected by their hairy legs. In every compartment of French railway trains, a notice was prominently displayed: 'Enemy ears are listening to you' – to the embarrassment of any traveller who seemed to be listening to the conversation of his fellow-passengers. In England wealthy people, who had installed concrete tennis courts before the war, were suspected of preparing gun-emplacements from which the Germans could bombard London. In most belligerent countries there was a mass internment of enemy aliens: only Austria-Hungary stuck to more civilized standards. The English shipped their aliens to the Isle of Man, which thus received a large population of German waiters and German brass bands – the latter a feature of pre-war English streets which now disappeared for ever. German shops were looted in every capital city; when the supply of these ran out, the looters passed on to any shop with a foreign-sounding name. In London young women paraded the streets, offering white feathers (symbol of cowardice) to any man still in civilian clothes. More practically-

41. The comforts of a haycart for arrested spies.

minded people toured the shops, stocking up with hams and cheeses against the famine which they expected at any moment.

The refugees were another disturbing element. All over Europe people fled before the advancing armies, trudging along beside carts laden with their household goods. Usually they could settle elsewhere in their own country – strangers indeed, but not foreigners. The Belgians had no remaining country to settle in, the little coastal strip was entirely occupied by the Belgian army. Over a hundred thousand of them arrived in England. They received at first a warm welcome. Later, things changed. The Belgians were resentful that the great British Empire had not protected them more successfully. English people were disappointed to find that most Belgians were ordinary folk of mixed character, not heroes. Belgians did not settle easily into English life; Belgian workers did not fit into English factories. In the end they were given a munitions town of their own in Northumberland, where Belgian street names, Belgian police, and even, strange to relate, Belgian beer gave them the illusion of being at home.

Yet, with all this upheaval, there was still general enthusiasm for the war. Pre-war animosities were stilled. All over Europe

42. Belgian refugees unwillingly at the seaside.

industries had never known such a freedom from strikes. In England the suffragettes abruptly ended their campaign of violence. The Futurists, who had caused almost as much upset in France, were now rejoicing at the music of the guns. Discontented nationalities were discontented no longer. The Irish volunteered as eagerly in southern Ireland as in Ulster. The Croats fought fiercely against the Serbs, their fellow South Slavs. Some Czech regiments surrendered to the Russians, from the good soldier Schweik's dislike of fighting, not from Slav solidarity. Revolutionary Socialists who had preached resistance to war were now propagandists for it. Even the few Bolsheviks in the Duma indicated that they would support the war so long as it was a genuine war of patriotic defence; this did not save them from being sent off to Siberia soon afterwards. Lenin, in his Swiss exile, was almost alone in opposing the war from the outset; and he did not do much except work in the library on his book, *Imperialism – the last Stage in Capitalism*. A few doubting voices were raised elsewhere. Bernard Shaw shocked British opinion by his pamphlet *Commonsense about the War*, in which he argued that the violation of Belgian neutrality was a mere pretext and that the real object of the war was to destroy a dangerous rival – it was the last spring of the old British lion. However, Shaw supported the war on these cynical grounds, and was soon an honoured guest at headquarters.

None of the statesmen who had blundered into war was discredited by his blunders. Asquith, Viviani, Bethmann, remained national leaders. Even silly Berchtold, who had started the whole thing, was not got rid of as Foreign Minister of Austria-Hungary until early in 1915, and then only at the order of Tisza, Hungarian Prime Minister. Tisza arrived in Vienna to tell the Emperor Francis Joseph that Berchtold was no good at his job. Berchtold said: 'Oh, do tell him. I tell him every day, and he does not believe me.' With this he vanished gratefully into obscurity, and spent the rest of his life writing memoirs which he did not complete. The generals who had failed to fulfil their confident promises of victory were discredited even less. Moltke indeed had gone, and Falkenhayn never became a public figure. Hindenburg more than occupied the vacant place. Joffre reigned supreme over the Allied line in France. The British people had unlimited faith in Kitchener, though his colleagues were soon more doubting. Even Sir John

44. Tisza contemplating the future of Hungary.

French was supposed for some time to be a great military leader. Nowhere did the people doubt that the war could still be won. Though the quick victory had not come off, the campaign of 1915 was expected to settle things. The generals doubted least of all. They had relied on mass, the sheer weight of men; now they asked for greater weight than before. They still thought in offensive terms, particularly on the Allied side. Therefore the new recruits were trained to believe that the bayonet was the decisive weapon. The generals turned down defensive weapons such as the machine guns, as though accepting them would be a confession of failure.

No one asked what the war was about. The Germans had started the war in order to win; the Allies fought so as not to lose. There were no clear war aims. Of course the French hoped to recover Alsace and Lorraine; the British were determined to liberate Belgium. But these were not enough in themselves; they were symbols of victory, not the reason why it was being pursued. Winning the war was the end in itself. Nevertheless the first campaigns changed the pattern of international relations. Before the war, most Germans regarded Russia as their dangerous enemy, and asked nothing of Great Britain and

46. *Canadian troops fix bayonets before going over the top.*

France, apart from a few colonies, except to be left alone. No German thought seriously of acquiring Belgium or north-eastern France. Now they were there; and the prizes further east seemed trivial in comparison. *Mitteleuropa* or the Berlin-to-Bagdad railway became the dream of a few professors in Vienna. Important Germans – great capitalists and leading politicians – wanted to keep their industrial gains in the west. The two Western Powers became the real enemy; and it was Russia who was now asked to leave Germany alone. Already some German statesmen were thinking of a compromise peace in the east, perhaps even giving Russia some reward at Austria's expense. The shift went further. Though the French army was the main obstacle in the west, the Germans believed that France, too, could be forced to a compromise peace, if she were not sustained by British money, British moral backing, ultimately by a great British army. Great Britain seemed to be wantonly interfering in Europe, in order to prevent unification under German leadership instead of being content with her Empire. She was now 'Enemy No. 1'. The 'Hymn of Hate' was directed against her; Germans looked forward to 'The Day' of her downfall. The British, on their side, had no

47. Fraternization on Christmas Day 1914. Photographs permitted only of officers.

difficulty in recognizing their principal antagonist. They believed that they were now fighting for their existence against their former German cousins. The King of England struck German princes off the roll of the Garter; and, a little later, changed his own German name to the English 'Windsor'. Thanks to the accident of the Schlieffen plan and its still more accidental result, the First World War turned into an Anglo-German duel.

Yet perhaps the peoples were less affected than the writers or politicians by these high speculations. On Christmas day in France firing stopped in the front line. British and German soldiers met in No Man's Land, gossiped, exchanged cigarettes. In some places they played football. They met again the next day. Then, after strong rebuke from headquarters, firing gradually started again. In the churches at home, prayers were offered for victory and for the slaughter of the men who were exchanging cigarettes. An English poet (J. C. Squire) wrote:*

> God heard the embattled nations sing and shout:
> 'Gott strafe England' – 'God save the King' –
> 'God this' – 'God that' – and 'God the other thing'.
> 'My God', said God, 'I've got my work cut out.'

* Reproduced by courtesy of Mr Raglan Squire and Messrs Macmillan & Co. Ltd.

48. *Death in the trenches, 1915.*

1915

On 2 January 1915 Kitchener had one of his gleams of insight. He wrote to Sir John French: 'I suppose we must now recognize that the French army cannot make a sufficient break through the German lines of defence to bring about the retreat of the German forces from northern France. If that is so, then the German lines in France may be looked upon as a fortress that cannot be carried by assault, and also cannot be completely invested.' No other military leader saw things so clearly; and Kitchener's vision soon faded. Contemporary military doctrine taught that an enemy must be defeated by attacking his forces at the strongest spot; and the strongest forces, both Allied and German, were obviously in northern France. The French were further hypnotized by the fact that 'national territory' was in enemy occupation. French generals and politicians believed that public opinion would revolt against a defensive strategy; and they shared this opinion. There had to be new offensives in France, even if the chances of success were small; and the French generals, nurtured on the doctrine that the offensive always succeeds, could not bring themselves to admit that it might fail. Something had gone wrong with the doctrine in 1914; they still thought it stronger than the facts.

The French dragged the British along with them. In theory the British Expeditionary Force was an independent army. In practice it followed Joffre's directive. Kitchener, despite his doubts, was embarrassed at the smallness of the British contribution; and tried to overcome it by an excessive loyalty in doing whatever the French asked. Besides, he foresaw a time when the British army would be stronger than the French; and he 'anticipated a call' then to become Supreme Allied Commander. He conformed to French wishes now so that they would conform to his wishes later. There was no formal consultation between the Allied governments. Sir John French had to find out Joffre's plans through his liaison officer at French headquarters. Joffre concealed his plans from the Russians; and the Grand Duke Nicholas concealed his plans, so far as he had any, from Joffre. Civilian ministers in every country dared not criticize the generals, or challenge them. For one thing, there was no one they could turn to for independent advice. The generals, though often contemptuous of each other

and still more of their Allied colleagues, joined in a con-
spiracy of silence against the civilians. Moreover, with the
nation in arms, any criticism of the generals would shake
national unity. Ministers everywhere stood aside, professing,
for want of anything better, a faith in the generals which they
sometimes felt. The French, unlike the British, had a revolutionary tradition of criticizing their generals. Some members of
the Chamber of Deputies, who had been mobilized on the outbreak of war, followed this tradition; but this of course forced
ministers and generals together.

In Great Britain the doubts started higher up. From the
first, some members of the Cabinet questioned the ability of
the generals to win the war. The deadlock in France strengthened
these doubts. It was no unreasoning prophecy to say that the
war on the Western Front would not be won by bodies of
infantry, however large, battering against each other. The
events of the following years proved that this prophecy was
correct. The critics went further, particularly the two pre-war
Radicals, Lloyd George and Winston Churchill. They questioned
not only the method of fighting in France, in which they were
right. They questioned the wisdom of fighting in France at all.
This was more speculative. They wanted to turn the German
flank, to find a way round, a back-door into Germany. The
hard fact, not made plain on the maps, was that there was no
such back-door except Russia; and Russia could not be
reached easily. North-eastern Italy, Salonika, the Dardanelles
led nowhere, or were, at best, doors firmly bolted by nature in
Germany's favour. The debate between Westerners and
Easterners ran on, one way and another, throughout the war.
The critics said to the generals with truth: 'You will not win
the war in France with these methods.' The generals answered
with equal truth: 'You will not win the war anywhere else.'
There was a deeper, less avowed argument. The generals
insisted that the British could defeat a German army millions
strong only by raising millions of their own, by becoming in fact
a military power of the Continental pattern. The critics wanted
to preserve the distinct character of 'old England', with a great
navy and a small professional army. They imagined that somewhere, somehow, sea power would enable them to pull off a
smart trick, a brilliant manoeuvre, defeating Germany on the
cheap both in money and men.

All the projected 'side shows' of the First World War had
this character. They were 'dodges' in a double sense. They

49, 50. The Grand Fleet ruling the waves.

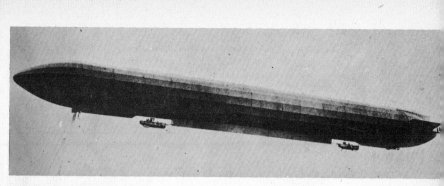

51, 52, 53. New weapons of war: gas, zeppelin, U-boat.

were ingenious; and they were designed to evade the basic problem – that the German army could be beaten only by an antagonist of its own size. Of course the side shows operated under peculiarly unfavourable circumstances. They were amateur in execution as well as in conception. Since the heretical politicians could not directly overrule the generals, their projects had to be additional to the main offensive in France, not instead of it – at a time when there were adequate supplies for neither. Nor could the politicians call on professional advice. Everything was settled hugger-mugger. There was no calculation, for instance, of the shipping needed to move men to the Mediterranean; no estimation of the equipment needed for an expedition to, say, Salonika or the Dardanelles. None of the politicians looked at a detailed map before advocating their 'side shows'. They were clearly ignorant that Gallipoli has steep cliffs, and Salonika a background of mountains. All the side shows were 'cigar butt' strategy. Someone, Churchill or another, looked at a map of Europe; pointed to a spot with the end of his cigar; and said: 'Let us go there.'

The side shows had a further motive, which could not be admitted to the allies of Great Britain and which was perhaps not even recognized by the protagonists themselves. They all took place outside Europe or on its fringe; though they would do little harm to Germany even if successful, they would bring gain to the British Empire. Deep down they sprang from the psychology of the old days when Great Britain was thought to be a purely imperial power, who did not care what happened in Europe. Even now, the defeat of Germany could be left to France and Russia, while Great Britain added to her Empire elsewhere, much as she had done during the Napoleonic War. This was exactly what the French suspected. The British, they complained, were collecting the spoils of Asia on the cheap, while they themselves were bleeding to death on the Western Front. The only way of lulling this suspicion was for the British to send more and more men to France, and to fight there with increasing obstinacy. Not only were the side shows kept short of men and material, and therefore less useful than they might have been. They themselves became a prime motive for a British mass army and mass slaughter in France, though they had been conceived in the first place to make these unnecessary. Such are the tangles produced by war, particularly by a war fought with allies.

The Germans behaved a little more sensibly during 1915. Schlieffen had landed them in trouble by his plan which was bound to fail; but at least his repudiation of frontal attacks saved them from further follies. Falkenhayn acknowledged that the Allied line in the west could not be turned; therefore he decided to stand on the defensive, and clear up the Russian front instead. In practice he had little choice. The Austrians could not hold their own even against a Russian army which had run out of supplies. The Germans had to go to the rescue. They hoped to knock Russia out of the war, or at any rate to push her armies so far east that they would cease to count. Falkenhayn was the only general on either side in the First World War who aspired to something less than decisive victory. He hoped that, with Russia defeated, the Western Allies would

accept a compromise peace in Germany's favour. Bethmann, the German Chancellor, was also convinced that there would be no decisive victory; but he dared not voice his opinion publicly for fear of discouraging the German people, and therefore waited passively until such time as they were disillusioned by events. During 1915 the German Government dropped some indirect hints to the Tsar Nicholas II that they would be willing to make peace on the basis of the *status quo*. He did not respond. He was loyal to his French allies with the obstinacy of a feeble man. Besides, like all other rulers, he feared that his authority would be shaken by anything less than total victory: then he might have to grant a real constitution or even be overthrown by a revolution. So Russia drifted on, incapable of winning the war, still more unable to escape from it.

There was another conceivable way of breaking the deadlock even if strategy failed. This was the invention of new methods or new weapons. The generals made no contribution here, or rather made the wrong one. Their only novelty was to blast a hole in the enemy lines by weight of bombardment; hence they demanded more and more guns and shells. They did not appreciate that this bombardment would so churn up the ground that the advance of the infantry after it would be slower than ever. Civilians and junior officers did better. In England ingenious minds devised a sort of armoured tractor, named – for reasons of security – the tank. It was not ready until 1917, though a few appeared in the Somme in 1916; and the generals used it wrongly. Scientists were already producing poison gas; and this was used by the Germans at Ypres on 22 April 1915. It had an initial success. Then, as each side acquired gas masks, the result was to increase the handicaps on the infantry, and so to slow things down further. Apparently no one had reflected that the attackers would have to wear masks against their own gas as soon as they advanced.

At the outbreak of war every army possessed a few aeroplanes, which were used for purposes of scouting. Later, fighters were produced to shoot down the scouts, and then more fighters to fight the fighters. The aeroplanes, moving slowly and held together by wooden struts, were too light to carry bombs in any number. They were not used for military bombardment until 1918, and the British were preparing an independent bombing force when the war ended. The Germans, however, started to bomb England in 1915. This was done at first with Zeppelins or airships, clumsy monsters which offered an easy target as soon as the British sent up fighter aeroplanes. When major Zeppelin raids ended in 1916, bombing by aeroplane followed. This caused great confusion in England, and great resentment. The British people had never experienced war at first hand. Public opinion demanded reprisals against the pilots, or even their execution. The whole country was blacked out at night; and work stopped everywhere when a solitary raider was sighted. The real effect was trivial by the standards of a later generation. Only eleven hundred English people lost their lives by attack from the air throughout the whole war.

The Germans had one other device which turned out the most dangerous of the lot. This was the U-boat or submarine. Here again its use had not been foreseen. Both German and British admirals thought of the submarine as an auxiliary to the main fleet, acting as scout or perhaps embarrassing the battleships. They did not suppose that it would be used against merchant ships. The German U-boats, along with the rest of their fleet, had a short cruising range. They could not keep up a blockade of the British Isles for long, particularly when the Straits of Dover were closed against them and they had to go round the north of Scotland. Nevertheless the Germans declared a blockade of the British Isles early in 1915. Unlike surface raiders, the U-boats could not give preliminary warning or take off the crews and passengers of the ships which they sank. They had to sink at sight, and leave crews and passengers to drown. This produced another great outcry against German barbarism. It had also a disastrous political effect. The greatest German stroke was to sink the British liner, the *Lusitania*, which was carrying some munitions, but also, among its passengers, a hundred Americans. The Germans were delighted:

55. Engineers in a U-boat worshipping their machine.

56. German medal to commemorate the sinking of the Lusitania.

medals were struck to commemorate the deed. American opinion was indignant. President Wilson protested strongly. The U-boats were the best propaganda for bringing the United States into the war on the Allied side. Some of the German leaders realized this, or at least Bethmann did so; they also appreciated that in 1915 they had too few U-boats to produce any decisive effect. They therefore offered to stop the U-boat war if the British would relax their blockade. The British refused. Later, after drowning more neutral Americans, the Germans limited the U-boat campaign all the same. But the damage had been done. Bethmann had to plead again, as he had done over the invasion of Belgium: 'Necessity knows no law.' Every Great Power acted on this principle, the Allies as much as the Germans. But the Allies, and particularly the British, managed to give the impression that they acted brutally or unscrupulously with regret; the Germans always looked as though they were enjoying it.

These themes, and many others, were only sketched lightly in 1915, like the lines of trenches across north-eastern France which had not yet taken on much thickness. Men still refused to believe that the war had turned out quite differently from

57. Turkish ships of the desert in full sail.

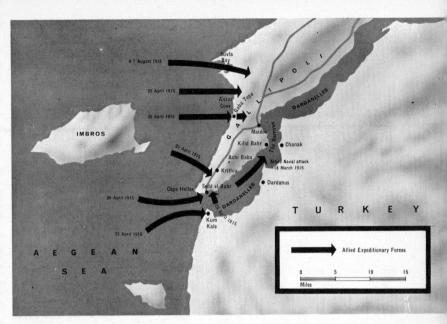

The following labels appear on the map:

6-7 August 1915 — Suvla Bay — 25 April 1915 — Anzac Cove — Baba Tepe — 25 April 1915 — GALLIPOLI — DARDANELLES — IMBROS — Maidos — Kilid Bahr — The Narrows — Chanak — 25 April 1915 — Achi Baba — Krithia — Allied Naval attack 18 March 1915 — Cape Helles — Sedd el Bahr — Dardanus — 26 April 1915 — DARDANELLES — TURKEY — Kum Kale — 25 April 1915 — AEGEAN SEA — Allied Expeditionary Forces — 0 5 10 15 Miles

The Dardanelles and Gallipoli.

what had been expected and had taken on a new unforeseen character. Joffre was for ever announcing that decisive victory would be achieved quite shortly; and Sir John French echoed his optimism. Yet strangely enough the episode which made 1915 for ever memorable did not spring from any of these famous leaders. It was provoked by the most despised of belligerents, the Turks. In October 1914 Turkey or, to give it a more grandiloquent name, the Ottoman Empire, entered the war on the German side. It is difficult to think of any rational motive for this act. The Turks could not possibly gain from the war even if Germany won; indeed the only remote chance of survival for their ramshackle Empire was that they should keep out altogether. But they had been alternately patronized or bullied by Russia and Great Britain for a century past; now the temptation to strike against both at once was irresistible. No sooner were the Turks in the war than all that remained of their army after the Balkan War of 1912–13 was sent off to attack Russia in the Caucasus; while a scratch force made a futile demonstration against the Suez Canal. The fighting in the Caucasus was an appalling campaign. It was conducted in mid-winter, far from supplies. Thousands of men were frozen into corpses overnight. When in January 1915 the Turks went

58. *Destruction at Gallipoli, 25 February 1915.*

reeling back, they had lost seventy thousand, out of a hundred thousand men.

The Russians had been hard pressed. On the last day of December 1914 Grand Duke Nicholas sent a desperate appeal to Kitchener for some British demonstration in the eastern Mediterranean which would distract the Turks. By the time the appeal arrived in London, it was already out of date: the Turks were in retreat from the Caucasus. However, Kitchener responded eagerly. Helping Russia seemed to him more useful than mere battering on the Western Front. Besides, as a former ruler of Egypt, he was worried, quite unnecessarily, that the Turks might attack the Suez Canal. Churchill was even more enthusiastic: here was the opportunity for a great amphibious action, using British control of the seas. Together Churchill and Kitchener urged an attack on the Dardanelles. Fisher, the First Sea Lord, also disliked the Western Front, though his private ambition was for an expedition to Sleswig – an idea not endorsed by anyone else. He had no faith in the attack on the Dardanelles, and ought to have known that there was an old staff opinion declaring that it could not succeed. Nevertheless he supported the plan, or at any rate failed to oppose it: partly out of loyalty to Churchill, his civilian chief, more because it would, in his opinion, involve the army and so eclipse the Western Front.

59. The men who failed at Gallipoli: General Sir Ian Hamilton and Admiral de Robeck.

Kitchener, however, was assured by Churchill that the navy could force the Dardanelles on its own. The British admiral in the Mediterranean was pushed into saying that the attempt might work. The British Government jumped at this wonderful solution: they could have an eastern campaign to turn Germany's flank, and yet continue to please Joffre by sending all the available British troops to France. On 19 February the British navy began a bombardment of the outer forts at the Dardanelles. There was hardly any resistance. British marines landed freely where a great army failed some months later. At this time a single division could have taken and perhaps held the Dardanelles.

The British thought that they had plenty of time. The great ships hung about in the Aegean for a month. Only on 18 March did they enter the narrow straits. The waters, it was supposed, had been swept free of mines. Again the forts were successfully bombarded. We now know that Turkish supplies of ammunition were exhausted; on the next day the British navy could have passed the Dardanelles unopposed. But on the way back, it ran into a line of mines which had been laid parallel with the shore, not – like the others – from coast to

60. Reconciliation in death: German and French dead side by side.

61. *Civilization triumphs again: after the gas attack.*

coast, and which the minesweepers had missed. Two British battleships, and one French, were sunk; three others were badly damaged. These were all old ships, due for scrap; and most of the ships, so scrupulously guarded now, were in fact scrapped the following year. But de Robeck, the British admiral, would not risk the loss of further ships. At this precise moment, it turned out that the risk was not necessary. Kitchener had decided that he could spare an army after all. Again, there was no rational calculation, no cool determination that the army in France should remain on the defensive. Kitchener merely felt that British prestige would be shaken if there were a failure at the Dardanelles. He sent for Sir Ian Hamilton, an old favourite from Boer War days, and sent him off with orders to capture Constantinople, saying: 'If you do, you will have won not only a campaign, but the war.' Hamilton left London without a staff, with no proper maps, and with no information later than 1906 about the Turkish defences. The force allotted to him had one regular division, the last remaining. Otherwise the troops were colonials and territorials, with no previous experience. The British army had never rehearsed landing on a hostile coast and had no equipment for this

purpose, despite all the talk about sea power. Everything had to be improvised from day to day.

Hamilton arrived just when de Robeck was depressed by the losses of 18 March. At once he offered to take over the campaign. The naval attack was called off and never renewed. When Hamilton examined the transports he found they had been loaded wrongly: useless stuff at the top, essential supplies at the bottom. The entire expedition, after alarming the Turks, weighed anchor, and retired to Alexandria where everything was repacked. It was away for more than a month. During that time, the Turks scraped together every available man, moved down all their reserves of ammunition. Forcing the Dardanelles was no longer an easy operation. Meanwhile Joffre was indignant that the Western Front was being neglected. To keep him in a good temper, Sir John French staged an attack at Neuve Chapelle on 10 March. The British army was short of shells. It could not afford a preliminary bombardment. The attack therefore took the Germans by surprise. The British infantry broke the German line – for the only time in the war. Nothing of any significance followed. The British hesitated to enter the hole which they had made. They waited for reinforcements; and, by the time these arrived, German reinforcements had arrived also. The gap was closed. The British went on battering to no purpose. When they gave up, the Germans battered in their turn, to equally little purpose. Neuve Chapelle lasted a mere three days, not much by later standards, but it was a warning of what was to happen again and again: success at the beginning which led nowhere, and then attacks going blindly on when they had obviously failed. The battle has another importance for English people. Sir John French, to conceal his failure, complained that he was short of shells. The Government in their turn blamed the munition workers, who were alleged to draw high wages and to pass their days drinking in public houses. Legislation was hastily introduced to restrict the hours when public houses were open and, in particular, to impose an afternoon gap when drinkers must be turned out. Those restrictions, still with us, rank with Summer Time as the only lasting effects of the First World War on British life. Anyone who feels thirsty in England during the afternoon is still paying a price for the battle of Neuve Chapelle.

Joffre was not discouraged by this British failure, nor by similar failures of his own. He went on demanding just one more attack, convinced each time that it would be decisive. These so-called battles have no meaning except as names on a war memorial: 50,000 French lost in February, 'nibbling' five hundred yards forward in Champagne; another 60,000 lost at St Mihiel; 120,000 lost in May near Arras. The British army tried new offensives at Festubert and Aubers Ridge, with casualties even higher in proportion. The spirit of the French army, already sapped by the disasters of August 1914, was worn down further. The first zest of the new British army was blunted. The Germans were inspirited by the success of their defensive. They attacked once only: at Ypres on 22 April where they first used poison gas. This was not only wicked. It was folly when the Germans had no force for a real offensive in the west. The attack achieved the desired result – a gap in the British line; but, as usual, the gap was stopped up when the gas cleared, and the German advance came to a halt. Sir John French sent up the casualty-list by insisting on counter-attacks. Smith-Dorrien, the army commander, protested. He was at once dismissed. Sir William Robertson, then French's Chief of Staff, announced this to him in the famous words: ' 'Orace, you're for 'ome.' A few days later French had to authorize withdrawal all the same. The affair gave a warning for the future. Those British generals who prolonged the slaughter kept their posts and won promotion; any who protested ran the risk of dismissal. By the middle of May the attacks had all petered out. Men and materials were alike exhausted; the decisive victory was as far off as ever; the Germans had not even been prevented from moving massive reinforcements to the Eastern Front.

Meanwhile Hamilton's preparations for attacking the Dardanelles were going slowly forward; and Turkish preparations to resist him were going forward also. By the time Hamilton was ready, he had five divisions, and the Turks six. Nevertheless the landings on 25 April took the Turks by surprise. At every point the men got ashore, sometimes with heavy loss, elsewhere without. Hamilton had designed his strategy well, but he was too polite to be a good general in the field. He was further weakened by his reputation as a 'poet' and literary man. He conscientiously refrained from spurring on his subordinates; and, during the landings, cruised up and down the coast on a battleship, out of touch with events. The unique chance remained open for twenty-four hours, or sometimes more; then it faded. The British troops were pinned down on the rocky shore, unable to reach the top of the hills and move into open country. The Turkish defenders crouched just above them. Once more, lines of trenches were drawn, in far worse conditions than in France. The British forces had no secure rear: only beaches exposed to Turkish shell-fire, and beyond them the sea. Everything, even water, had to be landed at night. There was no shade. Often the ground was too hard to find effective cover in. The attack on the Dardanelles was a brilliant idea in theory. But even the best idea brings disaster when it is carried out hastily and inadequately. The men and the shells which Sir John French frittered away in northern France to no purpose might have carried the Dardanelles and taken Constantinople. As it was, the war of movement had once more failed to come off. The British were as much stuck at Gallipoli as they were in France.

These two disappointments provoked a political crisis in Great Britain. Sir John French excused everything by his shortage of shells; and visitors to headquarters were briefed on the 'shell scandal'. Northcliffe, greatest newspaper proprietor of the day, determined to bring down Kitchener, the man responsible for supply. His attacks, though justified in every line, met with general disapproval; a copy of his paper, the

63. Lloyd George casts an expert eye over munition girls.

64. Girls promoted from chocolates to fuse-heads.

Daily Mail, was burnt on the floor of the Stock Exchange, thus paying a penalty for its lapse into truth. Lloyd George, inside the Government, was equally impatient with Kitchener; and so, outside, were Conservative backbenchers. In mid-May a second crisis exploded, this time over the Dardanelles. Fisher, who had never liked the project, grew increasingly restive as more battleships were sent to the eastern Mediterranean. He resigned without warning in a gesture of wild protest. Asquith, the Prime Minister, did not want a public row. He settled on coalition with the Conservatives in order to conceal the facts about both shells and the Dardanelles from the British people, another step towards the position that, if men knew the truth about the war, they would not go on fighting it. Thus ended the last Liberal Government of Great Britain, in a cloud of secrecy. Fisher disappeared. Kitchener did not – saved by the very Conservative revolt which was designed to turn him out. But his powers were reduced. Lloyd George took on the new job of Minister of Munitions.

This was a more significant event than the battles happening at the time. It marked for Great Britain, and soon for other countries, the beginning of a new sort of war. Until this moment, the British people had been treating the war as an extra, a luxury which they could have on top of their ordinary life. The War Office still ordered supplies on the peacetime scale; prices were determined by the law of supply and demand; the trade unions of skilled men kept women and unskilled men out of the engineering shops, with a cry of 'dilution'. Lloyd George made war seriously on the industrial front. He refused to accept the War Office estimate of future needs. He was equally contemptuous of the generals in the field. For instance, Lloyd George inquired how many machine guns were needed. Haig replied: 'The machine gun was a much overrated weapon and two per battalion were more than sufficient.' Kitchener thought that four per battalion might be useful, 'above four may be counted a luxury'. Lloyd George told his assistants: 'Take Kitchener's maximum; square it, multiply that result by two – and when you are in sight of that, double it again for good luck.' This feat of arithmetic gave sixty-four machine guns per battalion. Before the war was over every British battalion had forty-three machine guns and cried out for more. Again, the War Office refused to authorize production of the Stokes mortar, one of the best weapons of the war. Lloyd George got an Indian Maharajah to finance its production from his own pocket. Sometimes Lloyd George got results by threatening manufacturers with requisition; sometimes he let them make inflated profits – any method would do if it produced the goods. He persuaded the unions to drop their restrictions for the duration of the war, and did not scruple to promise them much improved conditions afterwards. Somehow the crying need for shells merged into the vision of a better Britain. The unions ceased to be instruments of class war. Their leaders became partners with the Government and with the bosses, except of course that they did not receive a cut from the increased profits.

Lloyd George went further in his search for more munition workers. Shortly after he became Minister of Munitions, the militant suffragettes staged a final demonstration under their leader, Christabel Pankhurst. They marched down Whitehall with the slogan: 'We demand the right to work.' Lloyd George gave them this right. Many hundred thousand women were brought into the shell factories. Others became typists in business and government offices: the male office-clerk vanished for ever. For the first time, women were earning their own living on a massive scale. They went into public houses, and paid for their own drinks. The girls in factories and offices needed more sensible clothes. Their skirts became shorter; they were no longer held in by tight corsets. Many of them cut their hair. Women took over as tram conductors. A little later, the armed forces started auxiliary services for women, who wore their own khaki uniform. There were women police. Other belligerent countries followed the same pattern, though none carried it so far as Great Britain. By the end of the war, it was no longer true that woman's place was in the home.

The change of government in England was intended to produce a more energetic conduct of the war. Instead it produced a long pause. British ministers stared helplessly at the expedition stuck on the rocky coast of Gallipoli, unable to decide whether to clear out, or to send more forces and try again. The armies of France were temporarily exhausted. Elsewhere things went on happening. The French disliked the Gallipoli affair. But they had their own plans for turning Germany's flank. Their first proposal was an expedition to Salonika in neutral Greece, from which aid could be sent to Serbia. Some Greeks were ready to enter the war. The Russians objected: they were afraid that the Greeks would get to Constantinople first and keep it for themselves. The French had

65. *Italian troops knock on Austria's back door.*

another idea: Italy should be brought into the war on the Allied side. Then Austria-Hungary could be attacked and so diverted from Russia. Privately the French feared for the future, if Italy husbanded her strength while they wore out theirs. Their motive for bringing Italy into the war was almost as much to weaken her as to gain an ally. Italy had been in theory the ally of Germany and Austria-Hungary when the war started. She at once declared that the war did not come within the alliance, and withdrew into neutrality. Both sides competed for her favour. The Germans offered her Austrian territory, Tyrol and Trieste, if she would remain neutral, to the impotent fury of the Austro-Hungarian Government. The Allies offered her much more – not only Tyrol and Trieste, but northern Dalmatia and a share of Asia Minor – if she would enter the war on their side.

The auction went on all through the winter of 1914–15. The revolutionary Socialist, Mussolini, who had formerly opposed all 'capitalist' wars, was hired by the French as a propagandist for fighting in defence of democracy. The romantic writer D'Annunzio and the Futurist Marinetti preached war as an extension of their literary theories. The great majority of the Italian people were indifferent and asked only to be left alone. But no one asked their opinion. The Allies carried the day. This was not so much because their concrete offers were greater, though they were. The journalists and politicians wanted war for its own sake. Italy claimed to be a Great Power, it was therefore ignoble that she should remain neutral when the other Great Powers of Europe were fighting. Italy had to prove herself the equal of Great Britain and France, and above the level of Sweden and Switzerland. War would invigorate and inspire her people: she would become great even if she were not great already. On 26 April Italy signed with Great Britain and France the secret treaty of London, promising to enter the war within a month; and receiving a promise of rich rewards in return. The Italian Chamber of Deputies had a majority in favour of neutrality. The agitators who wanted war organized mass demonstrations in Rome; a mob broke the windows of the Parliament House. The deputies voted obediently for war. On 23 May Italy declared war – against Austria-Hungary alone; she did not pluck up her courage to declare war against Germany until more than a year later.

Italy's entry into the war brought few of the advantages which the Allies had hoped for. The Italian navy cooperated

66. Italian soldiers find it heavy going.

with them in the Mediterranean, though it could not be relied on to stop Austrian submarines breaking out of the Adriatic. Economically Italy was a considerable burden. The British were already keeping France supplied with coal, since nearly all the coal mines in north-eastern France were behind the German lines. Now they had to supply Italy also. The Italian army had not recovered from the Libyan War of 1912. It had plenty of men, but little equipment and hardly any heavy guns. The supposed back-door into Germany through Austria-Hungary was virtually locked by nature. Italy was ringed around by mountains. The Austrians held the mountain line, and the Italians had to fight their way up from the plain. As well, if they tried to advance into Istria, they were threatened in the rear from south Tyrol, which stuck out as a salient behind them. The campaign in Italy repeated the story of the campaign in France, under worse conditions; a series of barren attacks which achieved nothing. Military experts count eleven battles of the Isonzo – eleven unsuccessful attempts to shake the hold of the Austrians on their mountain barrier. Of course Austro-Hungarian forces were kept engaged by this fighting; but nearly as many had been needed to garrison the frontier

67, 68, 69. Devotion and war on the Eastern Front.

even when Italy was neutral. On the other hand, fighting against Italy revived flagging spirits in the many nationalities of the Habsburg Empire. Few of them felt hostility to Russia; all resented Italy's stab in the back, and rejoiced that the dying Empire could still win victories somewhere.

The Italian politicians had rushed into the war largely in alarm that Russia was about to defeat Austria-Hungary. Unless Italy entered at once therefore, she would be too late. Great Britain and France, on the other hand, pushed Italy into war as a means of helping Russia. There was good reason for this, though the means proved ineffective. The Russians could make headway so long as they had to deal only with the army of Austria-Hungary – an empire even more dilapidated than that of the Tsar. In March 1915 the Russian army resumed the offensive in Galicia, and took the great fortress of Przemysl. This success strengthened Falkenhayn's determination to concentrate on the Eastern Front during 1915: if the Russian army were defeated decisively enough, Falkenhayn could face the Allies on the west in superior force and bring them, he hoped, to a compromise peace in Germany's favour. Throughout March and April troop trains rolled across Germany eastwards; Joffre's offensives did nothing to deter this shift of forces. Soon the German Supreme Command moved to the east also: Kaiser William II nominally the supreme warlord, Falkenhayn the real commander as Chief of the General Staff. This was a hard knock for the commanders in the east, Hindenburg and Ludendorff, who had previously had things all their own way. Now they were subordinates. They answered by criticizing Falkenhayn, producing rival plans to his, and blaming him for anything that went wrong.

Hindenburg and Ludendorff, occupying East Prussia, wanted to stage a sort of Schlieffen plan for the east. They would swing round behind the Russian armies, and encircle them. This had the additional advantage that Hindenburg and Ludendorff would get the credit. Falkenhayn had learnt from the failure of the original Schlieffen plan that forces moving on the outside of a circle went slower than forces falling back on a straight line; the Russians, he believed, would escape. After fierce argument, William II supported Falkenhayn. Whole divisions were taken away from Hindenburg, and sent south to stiffen the Austro-Hungarian army. On 2 May the combined forces attacked at Gorlice on a twenty-eight-mile front. The Russian line was thinly held. The infantry was

hardly trained; many were even without rifles, and had to
snatch them from the hands of their dead comrades. The
Russian front was blown apart. This was the only genuine
breakthrough on any front in the whole course of the war: the
only one, that is, so wide and deep that it could not be sealed
off. The Russians abandoned first Galicia, and then most of
Poland. They lost three-quarters of a million men in prisoners
alone, and more territory than the whole of France. Something
like ten million civilian refugees trailed along with the armies.
Yet there was no decisive victory. The Russians were falling
back on their supplies, inadequate though these might be;
the Germans and Austrians were marching away from theirs.
The very lack of railways which had hampered the Russian
advance now saved them in retreat. The weight of attack
which Falkenhayn used to win the breakthrough made it
impossible to move fast afterwards. The momentum of advance
slowed down. By September the Russians had built up a new
line – three hundred miles further east, but a line all the same.
Despite defeat, Russia was still in the war.

The Germans had still to keep a great army in the east.
Indeed they had to keep a bigger army than before merely to

70. '*V' Beach,
Gallipoli*.

control occupied Poland. Moreover Falkenhayn's victory made it more difficult to negotiate a compromise peace with Russia. Previously the Germans would have been content with the *status quo*. Now they wanted to keep some, if not all, of the territory which they had conquered. Here again the war manufactured war aims of itself as it went along. On the other side, the Russians now had something solid to fight for: liberation of the soil of Holy Russia. The spirit of their army actually improved. To inspire it further, the Tsar Nicholas II dismissed the Commander-in-Chief, the Grand Duke Nicholas (who was sent off to the Caucasus) and took command himself. This was a terrible blunder. Most rulers were supreme commanders in theory. Even President Poincaré, in his knickerbockers, was Commander-in-Chief of the French army. But the rulers had sense enough to keep out of the way. William II left everything to the Chief of Staff, though he hung about at headquarters. Nicholas II was incapable of command, yet would delegate it to no one else. Henceforward the Russian army drifted without a leader or a strategy, offering to the Germans only the shadow of a threat.

71. Suvla Beach: horses were indispensable even here.

The Allies in the West had done nothing to distract the

Germans while the Russians were suffering catastrophic defeat. Their armies had been exhausted by Joffre's futile offensives in May. He was still eager for fresh onslaughts. The new British Government wrangled over strategy among themselves. They were against further offensives until Kitchener's new armies were ready on a large scale in 1916. Moreover they felt that British prestige in the East would be badly damaged unless the attack at Gallipoli was pushed to a successful conclusion. On 5 July a conference of British and French ministers was held at Chantilly – the first attempt during the war to coordinate Allied strategy. Kitchener, the only Englishman present who spoke perfect French, dominated the proceedings. He seemed to have things all his own way: defence in France, attack in Gallipoli. Joffre remained silent, and apparently acquiesced. In reality, he won. Before the meeting, Joffre and Kitchener went for a quiet walk in the woods. Kitchener promised to support a new offensive on the Western Front in September, if the attack at Gallipoli were allowed to proceed first. Joffre closed the bargain.

All was now set for a new effort at the Dardanelles. Five more divisions were sent out to Hamilton, making thirteen in all; yet in the same period no less than sixteen new divisions joined the British army in France. The Turks had not wasted the long pause. They had increased their forces to sixteen divisions. Hamilton had asked for some younger energetic generals from France. He was told that none could be spared, and that he must take generals according to Army List seniority. He was thus provided with General Stopford, Lieutenant-Governor of the Tower, who had never commanded in wartime. The new attack was fixed for 6 August. Once more Hamilton took the Turks by surprise. At Anzac Bay one column got within a quarter of a mile of the ridge with only twenty Turks ahead of them. It then settled down to breakfast, and by the time it had finished, the ridge was bristling with rifles. At Suvla Bay 20,000 men were put ashore almost without loss; only a thousand Turks, without machine guns, barred their way. Here Stopford was in command. He did not go ashore. Instead he congratulated the men on their successful landing, and settled down to his afternoon nap. On shore, the men were told to relax; they went off to bathe, with no Turks between them and victory. Hamilton, as before, was too polite to interfere. Once more he cruised along the coast. Finally, in desperation, he called on Stopford, whom he found asleep.

*72. The trench
system from the
air, in theory.*

Hamilton urged immediate advance. Stopford said things must
wait until next day. Hamilton withdrew. On the following day
the British troops ashore dug defences. On 8 August they
attempted to advance. By then the Turks were too strong for
them. The attack at Gallipoli had failed – this time for good.
Stopford was recalled. The British army remained in its
impossible position, its supplies now interrupted by the
autumn gales. Hamilton still talked of victory. At home, in
England, his advice was discredited. Some ministers wanted to
withdraw; others talked of the blow to British prestige. At
Gallipoli men went on dying.

Joffre now presented his postdated cheque: he called for an
autumn offensive in France. When British ministers expostu-
lated, Kitchener replied: 'We have to make war as we must,
and not as we should like to.' In any case, he added, unless the
British gave full support, Joffre would be overthrown and the
French politicians would then make peace. Hence British
soldiers died so that France could be kept in the war. Joffre
was once more confident of success. This time there was to be
a combined offensive: one in Champagne on the right, the
other near Arras on the left. The Germans would be compelled

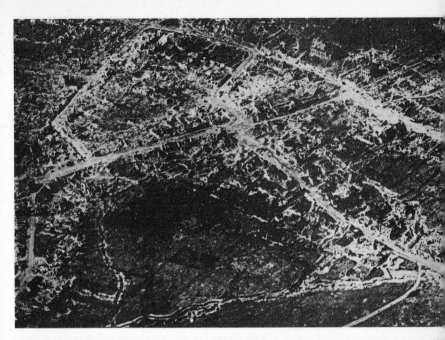

73. The town of Loos from the air, in practice.

to fall back beyond the Meuse, or possibly give up altogether. The French attacked in Champagne on 25 September. They made an alarming discovery. Though they overran the German front line, this brought no advantage. The Germans had a fully prepared second line behind it. The original thin trenches were, in fact, growing thicker: the front held by fewer men, the real defence stronger behind it and easier to reinforce. This defence in depth turned ordinary offensives into pointless slaughter. After three days the French attack was called off. The divisions of cavalry which had been waiting for the breakthrough returned once more to their billets. The French attack in the north stuck equally decisively.

Joffre laid down that the British attack must be made at Loos. French objected: it meant attacking across coalfields and through a wilderness of miners' cottages. Joffre insisted: he had chosen Loos as a spot on the map without considering whether it were suitable, and now he stuck to it. Kitchener ordered French to follow Joffre's directive. Haig, the army commander, was confident of victory, particularly as gas was to be used. But on the appointed day there was little wind and that in the wrong direction; as a result one divisional

74. *'Foxy' Ferdinand of Bulgaria and Archduke, later Emperor, Charles of Austria.*

75. *Serbian soldiers exhausted by retreat.*

commander, who insisted on releasing the gas, duly gassed his own men. However the British troops were running over with enthusiasm. On the right they broke through the German front line, and almost penetrated the second. Haig called for reserves. French, who was rightly jealous of Haig, had kept the reserves in his own hand. They were far in the rear. As they moved up, they tangled with troops coming out of the line. The official history says: 'It was like trying to push the Lord Mayor's procession through the streets of London, without clearing the route and holding up the traffic.' During this confusion the Germans counter-attacked. The British, in their turn, were threatened with a breakthrough. Then renewed deadlock. After a pause, the British renewed their attack to please the French, who had themselves stopped fighting. The offensive petered out early in November. The balance sheet was grim. The Allies made no gain strategically or even on the most limited scale; there had been simply useless slaughter. The British lost over 50,000 as against 20,000 Germans. The French lost 190,000 against 120,000 Germans. Yet Joffre was still cheerful. Even if he had not defeated the Germans, he was confident that he was wearing them down. One of these days

76. French infantry arriving at Salonika.

all the Germans would be killed, even if far more British and Frenchmen were killed in the process.

The autumn offensives in the west did not even distract the Germans from activity elsewhere. The position of Turkey was precarious despite the British failure at Gallipoli. Turkish munitions were running out; and the Germans could not send fresh supplies so long as Serbia stood in the way. Falkenhayn therefore determined to open the road to Constantinople by eliminating Serbia from the war. Large German forces were moved from the Eastern Front. As well, Bulgaria was drawn in. The Allies entered the auction for Bulgarian favour. They were at a disadvantage. Bulgaria coveted Macedonia which had been acquired by Serbia after the Balkan War of 1912–13. The Germans could cheerfully offer this; the Allies could only urge cession on Serbia, and the Serbs were unyielding. In September 1915 'Foxy' Ferdinand became secretly Germany's ally. Nevertheless the British and French governments made high-sounding declarations about the aid which they would send to Serbia. This was easier said than done. On 5 October one British and one French division landed at Salonika in neutral Greece – an act as unscrupulous in its way as the German invasion of Belgium. Two days later a German and an Austro-

The Balkans.

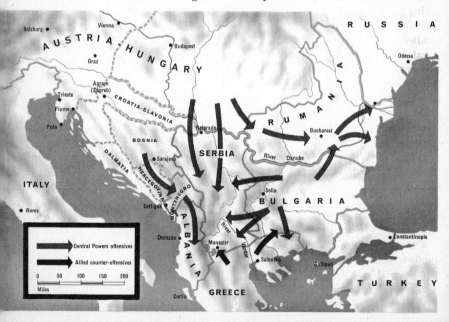

Hungarian army crossed the Danube. On 11 October the Bulgarians invaded Macedonia. Sarrail, in command at Salonika, tried to advance up the Vardar. The Bulgarians were too strong for him, and he was driven back. The Serbian armies were broken in pieces. The remnants retreated across the mountains of Albania, with King Peter in a litter. They reached the sea, and took refuge on the island of Corfu. Early in 1916 they joined the Allied forces at Salonika. Meanwhile the Austrians completed the record of success by conquering Montenegro and overrunning Albania.

The Allied expedition at Salonika had failed in its purpose. The British proposed to withdraw. It was now the turn of the French to insist on remaining; Joffre did this mainly to keep Sarrail out of the way, seeing in him a dangerous rival. For Sarrail, though not an exceptional general, was 'a good Republican'. Reluctantly the British acquiesced. New forces were sent to Salonika, reaching a total of nearly half a million men before the end of the war. They served no useful function except to keep occupied a Bulgarian army which had no intention of taking part in campaigns elsewhere. The Germans rightly called Salonika 'their largest internment camp' – half a million Allied soldiers locked up without even the trouble of taking them prisoner. But what should be done about the Dardanelles? Hamilton wished to make a new effort. He was recalled. Commodore Keyes offered to force the Straits by naval action. The admiral on the spot agreed. The British Government forbade it. Sir Charles Monro was sent out from France to survey the situation. Within twenty-four hours of arrival, he recommended immediate withdrawal. Kitchener could not bring himself to agree, though he knew there was no alternative. Once more British ministers wrangled – some fearing terrible casualties if there were an evacuation, others wishing to get rid of Kitchener.

Finally Asquith hit on a wonderful solution: Kitchener himself should be sent to inspect the Dardanelles, with a vague hope that he might never come back. For most British ministers now put the blame on Kitchener, quite unjustly, for the record of failure; yet it was essential to keep him as a symbolic figure – 'a great poster', Asquith's wife called him – for the sake of public opinion. Kitchener knew that he was being shunted out of power. However he went off loyally to the eastern Mediterranean. Once there he, too, reluctantly agreed that Gallipoli would have to be evacuated. But he refused to stay in the Near

77. Serb soldiers reach Corfu.

78. King Peter of Serbia experiencing the bitterness of defeat.

East. When he returned to London, he found that Asquith had
carried out a revolution in military affairs behind his back.
Hitherto Kitchener had run the war on land all alone, as
Secretary of State, with no expert advisers and consulting the
Cabinet only in the most general terms. Now Asquith brought
Sir William Robertson back from France, and made him Chief
of the Imperial General Staff on an entirely new basis. Robertson became the Government's sole adviser on strategy, and
the only man who could issue strategical directives to the
generals or could order the movements of armies. Henceforth
Kitchener and his successors as Secretary of State for War had
nothing to do with the war except to provide the men; and
even that was soon taken from them. For more than two years,
Robertson reigned supreme, sometimes a little harassed later
on by civilian ministers. During most of this time he had a free
hand over strategy – a little less free than Joffre had at the
height of his power, freer than Ludendorff ever had and of
course infinitely freer than any general had in any country
during the Second World War.

Sir William Robertson was the first British general to have
risen from the ranks; and he maintained a barrack-room

*79. Destruction
before evacuation :
stores are burnt
on 'A' Beach,
Gallipoli.*

roughness. He met heretical suggestions with the unvarying answer: 'I've 'eard different.' He told Lloyd George: 'It is a waste of time explaining strategy to you. To understand my explanation you would have had to have my experience.' Robertson had no idea how the war should be won except that it must be won in France. The reason for this was simple. France was the decisive theatre of war because the bulk of the British army was there; and the bulk of the British army was there because France was the decisive theatre of war. Like Joffre, Robertson held that the Allies were gamblers with the longer purse – their money being the lives of men. Sooner or later, German resources would run out. The calculation was false. The German intake of men reaching military age was more than enough to replace their losses until they, in their turn, wore themselves out by taking the offensive in 1918. Nevertheless Robertson went on preaching the offensive in France, though without hope that it would succeed.

The appointment of Robertson brought final decision about Gallipoli. Here was a 'side show', taking men away from France. Robertson insisted that it must be ended at once. In the last days of December, Suvla and Anzac Bays were evacuated; on 8 January 1916 Helles Bay was evacuated also. The withdrawal at any rate was a complete success. Not a man was lost, though great quantities of stores were left behind. The Gallipoli expedition was a terrible example of an ingenious strategical idea carried through after inadequate preparation and with inadequate drive. It would be futile to speculate what its success might have achieved: Turkey probably out of the war, an effective route for supplies to Russia, perhaps (though this is less likely) a new front opened against Germany. The consequences of failure are more obvious. Churchill, who was unjustly blamed for the whole affair, left the Government, and never recovered his reputation during the First World War. The Straits to the Black Sea remained closed. Russia was cut off from her western allies. Desperate attempts were made to develop the two ports of Archangel and Murmansk in the far and frozen north. Though supplies accumulated there, the defects of the Russian railway system made it impossible to shift them. Most of them remained uselessly stacked in warehouses until Russia fell out of the war. Moreover, the failure of Gallipoli provided an unanswerable argument for those, like Robertson, who believed in concentrating everything on the Western Front.

80. *Lord Kitchener with his keeper, Sir William Robertson.*

Any attempt to turn Germany's flank was abandoned. Yet side shows went on despite Robertson's disapproval; only they went on to little purpose. The Turkish Empire, though crumbling, kept two British armies busy – one in Palestine, the other in Mesopotamia. Clearly the Suez Canal had to be protected. Equally clearly, this could be done only by advancing beyond it. But there lay the desert of Sinai. It, too, must be crossed. Thus the British pushed into Palestine, their need of men growing ever larger. The expedition to Mesopotamia had also started as a measure of protection, this time of the British-controlled oil wells in Persia. Here, too, it was tempting to push on up the Euphrates. Then, with the withdrawal from Gallipoli, it was felt that success in Mesopotamia would do something to restore British prestige in the East. Hence there was an advance which turned to disaster in April 1916, when Townshend was surrounded at Kut and forced to surrender. After this, British prestige had to be restored once more. Before the end of the war 600,000 men were engaged in Mesopotamia; 500,000 in Palestine; to say nothing of another half million at Salonika. No doubt they were collecting future plums for the British Empire. None, except those at Salonika

81. Turkish artillery in Mesopotamia drawn by oxen.

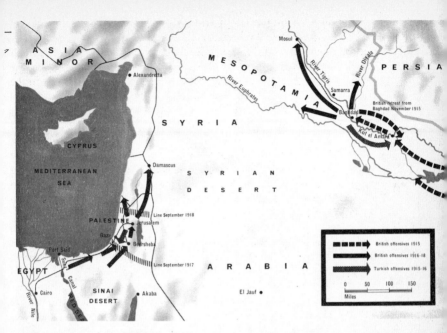

Mesopotamia.

at the end, contributed anything to the defeat of Germany.

Kitchener was not the only leader shaken by the failures of 1915. Sir John French, too, was a victim. His offensives had achieved nothing; and, to make matters worse, he had blamed Haig for the muddle over reserves at Loos, which was largely his own fault. Haig had been assiduous in expounding French's defects. He spoke of them to Asquith and to other distinguished civilians, whom he entertained sumptuously at his headquarters. He wrote constantly to the king, with whom he had long been on cordial terms. George V said: 'If anyone acted like that, he would at school be called a sneak.' However Haig got his way. In December 1915 French was recalled, and Haig became Commander-in-Chief of the British army in France, a post which he retained until the end of the war. Haig had a fine appearance, and a stern devotion to duty. Though he had no more idea than French how to win the war, he was sure that he could win it. Divine help would make up for any deficiencies on his part. This unshakeable confidence, combined with his influence at court, enabled Haig to survive a long record of failure and to emerge in the end victorious. Not that Haig was a mere courtier. He was a master of railway timetables, deploying divisions as skilfully as any general

82. *He relied on the divine help, became an earl and received £100,000 from parliament: Field-Marshal Sir Douglas Haig.*

83. French generals suffering from under-nourishment. In centre, *Joffre*.

of his time. His strategical judgements were sound within the framework of the Western Front, though he lacked the technical means for carrying them to success until almost the end of the war. A later generation may feel that Haig should have stood on the defensive and waited for the tanks. The French would not have tolerated this before 1917. The British public would have been still more indignant. A defensive strategy would have opened the door to talk of a compromise peace, against which even the civilian ministers who criticized Haig were sternly resolved. Haig had to do what he did; and, though he did not succeed, no one better was found to take his place.

Heads were falling in France also. Here it was the failure to help Serbia and to keep Bulgaria out of the war which aroused indignation. Delcassé, the Foreign Minister, resigned; Viviani's Government of 'sacred union' fell. Another collection of drab politicians, under the great orator Briand, took its place. Things were moving more seriously under the surface. The Chamber of Deputies refused to be denied any longer all say on the conduct of the war. Deputies visited the front, cross-examined generals, growled at Joffre's claim to be a war-dictator. Joffre himself was a skilful politician, though hardly an inspired general. He flamboyantly dismissed some of his subordinates, and listened patiently to visiting ministers. Moreover he invented a brilliant justification for his own existence: he alone had the prestige and influence to dominate France's allies, particularly to keep the British faithful to the Western Front. His critics accepted this argument. In this curious way, the French, who had little faith in Joffre, kept him as Commander-in-Chief because they thought that this would please the Allies; and the Allies, who also had no great faith in Joffre, conformed to his wishes because they thought that this would please the French.

On the other side of the lines, the German leaders had been more successful and were less open to criticism. Falkenhayn had won the biggest battle in history against the Russians, if one judges simply by size; he had overrun Serbia and opened the road to Constantinople. Yet he, too, was in trouble. Alone among the supreme commanders of the First World War, he did not expect total victory. He appreciated that now, at the end of 1915, Germany was no nearer achieving final success than she had been at the beginning. It was fatal for him that he could never breathe unquestioning confidence. He was, in fact, too sensible a man to hold his own in wartime. Moreover he had bitter enemies. His victories on the Eastern Front were won at a high price: they turned Hindenburg and Ludendorff against him. The two men were furious at having to conform to someone else's plan, particularly when they had to hand over troops to the front further south and did not get the credit for victory. They blamed Falkenhayn for the failure to knock Russia right out of the war; and were resolved to overthrow him. They had a tremendous asset. Hindenburg had become the symbol of victory for the German people – Kitchener and Joffre, as it were, rolled into one. He had only to threaten resignation; and Falkenhayn would go. The time was not yet, but it was coming. Falkenhayn could not face another year of rows with Hindenburg and Ludendorff. He decided that the great effort of 1916 must be in the west – justifying this decision with good technical reasons, but really wanting to escape from his two terrible rivals. In the late autumn of 1915, trains bearing William II and the Supreme Command rolled once more westwards.

The year 1915 thus produced a curious pattern. None of the generals except Falkenhayn had any great success to boast of;

*84. Collaborators:
the Polish Council
of Regency takes
service under the
Germans.*

yet in every country the military leaders, except paradoxically
Falkenhayn, increased their reputation. Kitchener, Joffre, and
Hindenburg personified the will to victory of their respective
countries. Public opinion, whipped up by the newspapers and
by sensational writers, turned them into demi-gods. Every
loyal citizen was expected to have unquestioning faith in these
great military leaders. Nearly all did so. There was, as yet,
hardly a flicker of discontent or discouragement in any belligerent country. In Ireland there was a nationalist minority
who believed that England's peril was Ireland's opportunity.
There was a lack of enthusiasm for the war among the Czechs
in Austria-Hungary. Here and there a few Socialists and
Radicals hinted that the war should end in a compromise peace.
No one heeded them. Anything short of complete victory was
regarded as an intolerable affront to national honour. Yet the
peoples still felt that they were fighting a defensive war for the
freedom and security of their homes. Most of the armies were
fighting on their own soil, or that of their allies. Only the
Germans held large areas of occupied territory – Poland in the
east, Belgium and north-eastern France in the west. Poland
had previously been oppressed by Russia; now it was

administered by Germans, and the Poles did not notice much difference – if anything there was an improvement. Indeed the Germans talked of 'liberating' Poland, and of re-creating an independent Polish state. Belgium was the only part of Europe which had a 'resistance' in the First World War. Even this was on a small scale. The Germans were too strong on the ground. There was no chance of a guerrilla war, and very little sabotage. The Belgians could not do much more than assert their continuing existence. They attracted much sympathy, particularly from neutral America. Herbert Hoover, the later President, organized food supplies and relief for Belgium which was allowed to pass the British blockade. Soon there were charges that the Germans were perverting this relief to their own use, and the British blockade was reimposed. Even the Belgian resistance was by no means solid. It came entirely from the French-speaking part of the population, the Walloons. The Flemings regarded the Germans as next door to liberators, and were far from enthusiastic when the Allies returned at the end of the war.

The civilian rulers were pushed aside in every country, and were often glad to shelter behind the military leaders. Not that they shared the popular devotion of the generals. Many ministers had doubts whether the war could be won by going on in the old way, but they were at a loss what else to do. Behind the scenes they listened to criticism of the generals in command by generals who were out of work, but it was difficult to believe that the running of the war would be basically changed by substituting one set of generals for another. No civilian statesman contemplated taking over the direction of the war himself as Churchill and Roosevelt were to do in the Second World War. Many ministers believed that their best contribution to the war was to keep out of the way, while the soldiers got on with the fighting. Asquith believed this in England; Bethmann believed it in Germany. Some ministers, more practically minded, concerned themselves with the production of munitions – the war on the home front as it was called. In England Lloyd George did more than this. He tried to win the backing of the factory workers and keep them from striking. His oratory ended a strike of South Wales miners in July. He was less successful at Glasgow, where on Christmas Day 1915 an audience of three thousand shop-stewards refused to hear him. The Socialist paper, *Forward*, was banned for giving a correct account of the meeting.

85. Herbert Hoover (right) provides and finds food relief in Belgium.

86. Lloyd George, a little apprehensive, on Llandudno pier.

The most startling political development of the year was the move towards compulsory military service in Great Britain. This was not due to any shortage of men. On the contrary, more volunteers were still coming forward than could be equipped. Parliament and the politicians wanted to give the impression that they were doing something active to aid the war; and conscription seemed the way to do this. Popular clamour insisted that 650,000 'shirkers' lay hidden. In January 1916 compulsory military service was carried for single men. This was a tremendous breach with tradition. Great Britain entered into direct competition with the military Powers of the Continent instead of relying on her sea power. The Liberal party was expected to split over the question, but conscription went through with hardly a murmur. Voluntary recruiting stopped. The compulsory call-up proved disappointing. Instead of revealing the 650,000 shirkers, it produced a million and a half claims for exemption from men who were performing essential work in industry. Conscription also produced conscientious objectors: few in numbers, five or six thousand in all, but adding the new word 'conchie' to the English language, and bringing home to people for the first time that it was possible to object to the war on high moral grounds. The debate on what the war was about was at last beginning. In Germany, at much the same time (December 1915), some twenty Social Democrats broke away from the official party, and voted against the war credits. Early in 1916 the Social Democratic party split formally into two. The war was challenged, at any rate in a limited circle.

The governments however had not got far in setting down their war aims, defensive or otherwise. Victory, it still seemed, would provide the war aims of itself. If the Germans won, they would obviously hang on to some of their conquests both west and east. If the Allies won, they would recover their national territory, and as yet no one talked of dismembering Germany – even defeating her was far off. There was more definition of aims in regard to lands outside Europe. The future of Turkey provided endless material for discussion. The Germans had opened the road to Constantinople by conquering Serbia; indeed their road ran without interruption all the way to Bagdad. This looked impressive on the map. 'Berlin-to-Bagdad' seemed to have become a reality. One enterprising German of progressive views announced that the future lay with *Mitteleuropa*. Many people in Allied countries believed

87. *The war broke his heart: Keir Hardie addresses a peace meeting in Trafalgar Square.*

88. Conscientious objectors cultivating the soil on Dartmoor.

that they were faced with a deliberate German plan of this kind. There was not much to it. The Germans sent some military supplies to Turkey, just enough to keep her going. But the railways through the Balkans and Asia Minor were a ramshackle affair, too slow and too badly equipped to act as the backbone of a real economic union. The Germans never drew supplies of any value from Turkey. They failed even to coordinate their economic system with that of Austria-Hungary, and watched the mounting confusion in their ally with casual indifference. *Mitteleuropa* was a myth, the geographical dream of a few professors. It was not a German war aim, nor even a German war method.

The Allies took the affairs of the Ottoman Empire more seriously. The three great allies – France, Russia, and Great Britain – had been in conflict over this question for nearly a century, and sometimes at war. It might soon stir suspicion between them again. The Russians took alarm early in 1915 when the Western Allies were planning the attack on the Dardanelles. They demanded firmly that Russia should be promised Constantinople and the Straits. The British had no objection so long as they could keep control of Egypt. The

French objected but had to give way. In April 1915 the promise was given. This was the first of the secret treaties which were to cause much scandal and disillusionment when they were made known. Critics could allege later that Great Britain and France were fighting the war in order that Russia should have Constantinople. This was not true. The promise was given in the hope of avoiding future quarrels, not as a prize of war. But it looked bad all the same. The British and French also tried to settle the future of the rest of the Ottoman Empire. The French complained that their soldiers were fighting and dying on the Western Front, while the British were planning to run off with all Turkey-in-Asia. To quieten this not-unjustified suspicion, the British promised that the French should have Syria. Unfortunately, other British agents were tempting the Arabs into the war by the promise that all the Arab lands of Turkey, including Syria, should become an independent national state. Still, one way or another, Turkey-in-Asia was being partitioned on paper – another plan for avoiding future quarrels which could easily be mistaken for a war aim. This was perhaps the oddest outcome of 1915. The Gallipoli expedition had been a failure. What was more, it determined that the Turkish Empire would never again become the decisive theatre of war. Yet at the same time, the Gallipoli expedition, by provoking the secret treaties of partition, left the impression that the Allies were fighting for the spoils of Turkey, not for great principles. No doubt the impression was wrong. All the same, it turned out difficult to apply the great principles; and easy to accumulate the prizes of empire. The oil wells of Mosul existed. But how exactly could one end war or make the world safe for democracy?

89. *Sir Douglas Haig sells an offensive to Lloyd George, Joffre underwriting, Albert Thomas not buying.*

1916

Though four Great Powers were at war against Germany, there had been so far little alliance except in name. There was no exchange of information, no coordination of plans. In the United States, British and French agents bid against each other for American supplies. Now there was an effort to improve things. On 6 December 1915, a military conference of all the Allies was held for the first time. Joffre presided at his Chantilly headquarters. He had become a great man – not only presiding over the Allies, but generalissimo of all the French armies. The Allied conference made a wide strategical decision for the coming year: there were to be simultaneous offensives against the Germans on the three main fronts – Western, Eastern, and Italian. Nothing much came of this decision. There was no proper exchange of timetables; the Italians could not mount an offensive large enough to distract the Germans; the Russians were beyond long-term plans. Joffre however remained unperturbed. He had no real interest except in the Western Front, and there he had got what he wanted. Henceforth, it was to become the focal point of British, as it had always been of French, strategy.

On 29 December Joffre had a more private meeting with Haig, who had just become Commander-in-Chief of the British forces in France. Earlier on, Haig had sharply criticized the offensives conducted by Sir John French. Once in supreme command, his views changed. He became convinced that the offensive could succeed. The British army in France was growing into a mighty force, as Kitchener's recruits were sent over. There were 38 British divisions in France at the beginning of 1916. The French had 95 divisions, making, with the Belgians, a grand total of 139 divisions against 117 German. Nineteen more British divisions arrived by July. Haig had always a favourite strategical idea: to attack Flanders and then 'roll up' the Germans from the north. Joffre did not like this idea. He doubted whether the British would fight hard enough unless he had them under his own hand; and for this a combined offensive was necessary. Joffre therefore pointed to the Somme, the spot where the British and French lines joined. This was a strange choice. There was no great prize to be gained, no vital centre to be threatened. The Germans, if pressed, could fall back to

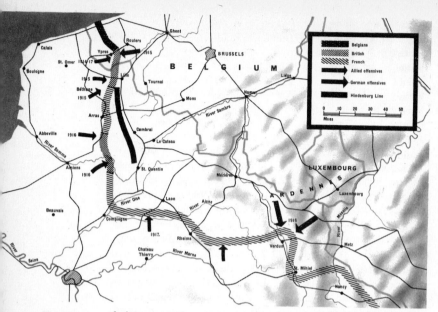

*The Western
Front: 1915–17.*

their own advantage, with better communications and a shortened line. Joffre did not care. The great thing was to pull the British into heavy fighting. Maybe Joffre hoped to stage something like the German breakthrough at Gorlice in the previous year; more probably he thought that heavy fighting was enough in itself – it would kill a lot of Germans. Haig did not defend his own plan. He loyally conformed to Joffre's strategy as Kitchener had instructed him to do.

Joffre and Haig imagined that they had plenty of time. They would wait until the middle of the year when the British soldiers would be better trained. Then forty French divisions would attack south of the Somme and twenty-five British divisions to the north of it. The German lines would be battered to pieces by a great weight of shell. The infantry would occupy the empty German positions. The cavalry would go through. This plan was never executed. Falkenhayn, too, had a plan, and got his blow in first. He did not believe that the war could be won on the Eastern Front. More victories there would merely draw the Germans deeper and deeper into Russia without destroying the Russian armies. Great Britain, he told William II, was 'the arch enemy, the heart of resistance against Germany'. She could be brought to her knees only by unrestricted submarine warfare; but for this the Germans had not yet enough

U-boats, and they shrank also from offending the neutral United States. The British therefore should be deprived of their Continental ally. Falkenhayn knew something of the great French losses and of their dwindling reserves. He therefore proposed to bleed the French white. Then France would fall out of the war, and the British would be driven to a compromise peace. This was not strategy. It was a policy of attrition, just like that of Joffre and Sir William Robertson, but more scientifically calculated. Falkenhayn did not seek a spot where victory would bring him strategical advantage. He wanted only a symbol which would be a challenge to French pride. The symbol was obvious and waiting for him. It was the famous fortress of Verdun.

Verdun was at the head of an awkward and useless salient in the French line; from any detached point of view the French position would have been stronger without it. Nor was it any longer a fortress. The rapid fall of Liège and of Namur at the beginning of the war had convinced Joffre that fortresses were useless; and Verdun had been stripped of its guns. The French people did not know this. For them Verdun was still a cornerstone of their defence, barring the road against the Germans. Joffre had ample warning that Verdun was to be attacked, ample warning also that its defences were in a bad state. There was not even a second line of trenches. In Paris, deputies back from the front raised the alarm in the Chamber. Gallieni, now Minister of War, inquired of Joffre what truth there was in these reports. Joffre replied by demanding the names of the informants, so that they could be punished. Nothing was done to strengthen Verdun. On 21 February 1916 a fourteen-inch shell exploded in the Archbishop's Palace at Verdun. It was the signal for the German attack, and the first of the tremendous bombardments which were to characterize 1916. The French line was battered by a weight of metal such as the world had never known before. The French defences east of the Meuse began to sag. Joffre sent little aid. He refused to take the German attack seriously. In any case, he would not allow it to interfere with the preparations for his own attack on the Somme later.

Briand, the French Prime Minister, was less calm. He had protected Joffre from criticism in the Chamber. He appreciated clearly that the fall of Verdun would be followed by the fall of his Government. On the evening of 24 February Briand motored to Chantilly. Joffre was already in bed asleep. Briand insisted on his being pulled out of bed – for the only time in the war. Staff officers tried to explain that Verdun was of no importance; indeed they would be glad to be rid of it. Briand, usually so conciliatory, lost his temper. He shouted: 'You may not think losing Verdun a defeat, but everyone else will. If you surrender Verdun, you will be cowards, cowards, and I'll sack the lot of you.' Joffre, still apparently half-asleep, let the storm blow on his subordinates. Then, opening his eyes, he said softly: 'The Prime Minister is right. I agree with him. No retreat at Verdun. We fight to the end.' A strange scene. Joffre had been on the point of making a sensible decision for the first time. The political chief intervened, again for the first time; and Joffre made the wrong one. The French fell into Falkenhayn's trap.

Pétain, the only French exponent of the defensive, was placed in command at Verdun. Every inch was contested. Between 21 February and the end of June, when the fighting died away, no less than seventy-eight divisions were fed into the mincing machine of Verdun. The Germans had secure communications behind their line; the French only one road, the 'sacred way', which was under German fire. Along this road 3,000 lorries passed and repassed every day. Without the automobile engine, Verdun could not have been saved. It was saved

90. Briand: he tried to win first war, then peace, by talk.

at the cost of the French army. The defence of Verdun shattered the French fighting spirit, and brought it to the verge of mutiny. So far Falkenhayn's calculation proved successful. But the Germans, too, paid a heavy price. Just as it was impossible to convince French opinion that Verdun was not worth saving, so it soon became impossible to convince German opinion that Verdun was not worth taking. The Germans imagined that they were fighting for a great prize, and ceased to count the cost. The German Crown Prince theoretically commanded the armies attacking Verdun; he wanted a dazzling success for the sake of imperial prestige. In vain Falkenhayn preached economy and the slaughter of Frenchmen by artillery fire. German troops, too, were soon being fed ruthlessly into the cauldron of destruction. German casualties mounted; those of the French grew relatively less. By the end of June, when the fighting died away, the French had lost 315,000 casualties, the Germans 281,000. This was the only offensive on the Western Front where the offensive cost less than the defence; it cost plenty all the same.

Verdun was the most senseless episode in a war not distinguished for sense anywhere. Both sides at Verdun fought

91. Marshal Pétain (at ease) *and French generals at Verdun.*

92, 93. *French soldiers in the fortresses of Verdun.*

94. A trench, once German, now French.

95. A German gun batters Verdun.

literally for the sake of fighting. There was no prize to be gained or lost, only men to be killed and glory to be won. The conflict at Verdun had a peculiar intensity. At some time during these four months no less than 115 divisions were crammed in by one side or the other on a front that was rarely more than five miles wide. The old forts, though neglected, added to the strange concentration. Men within them could defy all except the heaviest bombardments. Often the fighting went on within the forts themselves. The results nearly came up to Falkenhayn's expectation. The spirit of the French army was broken, and many units were on the brink of mutiny. On the other hand, the French held Verdun; and this had an inspiring effect on all those who had not fought there. Pétain had promised: 'They shall not pass.' They had not passed; therefore Verdun seemed a French victory. The defence of Verdun made Pétain's reputation. A colonel at the beginning of the war, he became a Marshal of France after it, and ultimately Head of the French State – all because of Verdun.

During the bitter fighting, Joffre sent out agonized cries for help to his allies. Haig agreed that the British should extend their share of the line. After much dispute, he agreed to advance the date of the coming offensive from 1 August to 1 July; more he would not do. The Italians promised to undertake an offensive, and made some attacks on the Isonzo front. Conrad, the Austrian commander, took the opportunity to break into their rear from south Tyrol. On 15 May the Italians, too, were calling for help. If Conrad had had support from some of the divisions which Falkenhayn was squandering at Verdun, the Austrians might well have broken out into the north Italian plain, and destroyed the Italian armies. As it was, the Italians, too, were in urgent need of assistance.

Only Russia could respond. The Russian position had been improved by the great retreat of 1915. They had a shorter line and better means of communication. Their army, too, was remarkably improved. It was always easy for them to replace the losses of men. The armament factories, now on a war footing, turned out abundant supplies, and the army was better equipped than it had been when the war began. Of course this was achieved at terrible cost. Everything was sacrificed to the army. Before the war Russia had exported wheat on a large scale. Now there was a shortage of food in the towns as the peasants were dragged off to the front. The administration was too clumsy and too corrupt to organize rationing properly. The railway system on which Russia depended was devoted to feeding and supplying the front – particularly to feeding the two million horses. Elsewhere the railways were on the point of collapse. Hunger mounted; and discontent with it. There were strikes all the time, without any recognized leaders. Yet the Tsar Nicholas II remained absolute ruler, rejecting all suggestions of reform and relying on the repressive power of the police and the Cossacks.

The Russian general staff, too, had their plan for 1916. Like most other plans, it consisted of attacking the enemy at his strongest point. The Germans were a more formidable foe than the Austrians; therefore the Russian offensive was to be directed against them. One Russian army was to attack in the north, another in the centre towards Warsaw. Both offensives were prepared with the elaboration usual during the First World War and with the blunders usual among the Russians. Masses of men were concentrated; there were prolonged bombardments to destroy the enemy line; copies of Russian plans fell into enemy hands. The Germans received full warning, and took full precautions. The offensives were a failure; they did not even relieve the pressure on Verdun. The Russian soldiers were shot to pieces for no purpose at all. The Russians lost five to every one German. When a further appeal came from Italy, the Russians had no prepared offensive to offer. Brusilov, the commander in the south, was ready to act without preparation. He had been indignant at being left out of the earlier plans. Now he stumbled on a new strategy more because he had to than from any conscious grasp. There were no concentrations of troops, no preliminary bombardments, hence no warnings to the enemy. On 4 June Brusilov's army simply attacked at twenty different points, wherever it happened to find an opening. The Austro-Hungarian front collapsed. Within three weeks the Russians took a quarter of a million prisoners. But Brusilov had no reserves. These were all in the north; and, since most Russian railways ran east to west not north to south, the reserves could not be moved in time. Besides, Brusilov's colleagues at headquarters were jealous of his success. Falkenhayn, on the other hand, sent seven divisions which he had intended for Verdun. When Brusilov attempted a further advance, he ran up against a hard German resistance. Then the Germans struck back. Brusilov retreated; and in the end paid the higher price. Thanks to his offensive the Russian armies in the south suffered over a million casualties.

96. General Brusilov, wounded, in bed.

The 'Brusilov offensive' was a remarkable achievement all

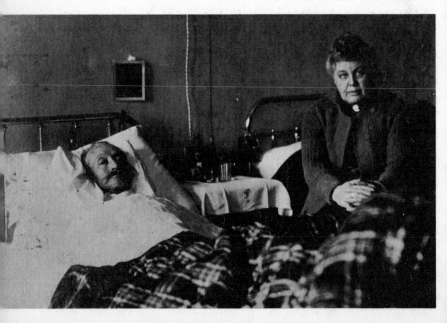

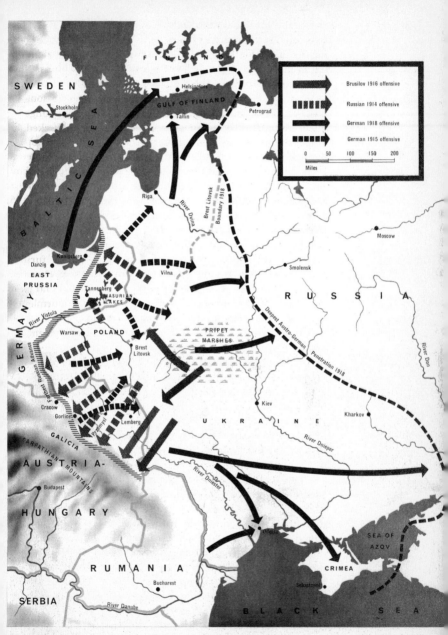

The Eastern Front.

the same – the only successful operation in the First World War to be named after an individual general. It succeeded by defying the rules. It failed when it conformed to the rules by attempting to push further on the same line of advance. The Germans learnt from Brusilov's success when they took the offensive in 1918; they did not learn from his failure, and repeated his mistake. The Brusilov offensive had great political consequences. It marked the moment when the armies of Austria-Hungary lost their fighting spirit. Unity, cohesion, loyalty vanished; and from this time Austria-Hungary was kept in the war by German power. The Habsburgs were not the only ones ruined by the Brusilov offensive. The Romanovs were ruined too. The Russian losses in Galicia were the final strain which cleared the way to revolution in the following year. As for Brusilov, he did not forgive the failure of the Tsar and of headquarters to support him. Two years later he was serving more happily under Trotsky.

Maybe the Brusilov offensive helped to take the pressure off Verdun. This was slackening in any case. Falkenhayn viewed the mounting German casualties with dismay. In mid-June he stopped further supplies to the front at Verdun. Thereafter the battle ran down of itself. It is often claimed that the British offensive on the Somme was launched in order to relieve Verdun. This is not true. The attacks at Verdun had stopped before the British offensive started, though the preparations for this offensive may have helped to stop them. The essential motive for the offensive on the Somme was quite other. Haig had come to believe that here was the spot where the war could be won. This belief was not shared by Sir William Robertson, the Chief of the Imperial General Staff. However, being junior to Haig in the army list, he loyally conformed to Haig's enthusiasm. The belief was not shared by Joffre; he had faith only in attrition, the more so on the Somme in that the British would pay the price on the Allied side. The belief was not shared by Rawlinson, the army commander in charge of the offensive; he, too, stifled his doubts and then, with equal rigidity, stifled the doubts of his own subordinates. The ordinary British soldiers, most of whom had no experience of previous fighting, imagined that they were about to win a great victory. This unreasoning faith was the link which bound them to Haig, the Commander-in-Chief whom they never saw.

The Somme had no longer any purpose as a field of battle. No strategical prize would be gained even if there were a great

97. British soldiers waiting to move up at the Somme.

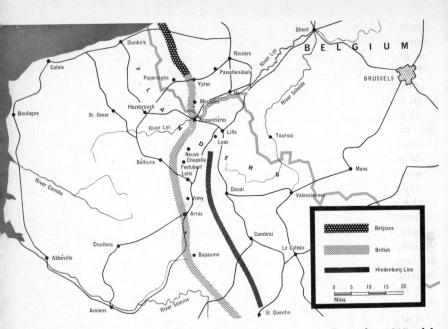

The northern sector of the Western Front.

advance. The Somme had been chosen in December 1915 solely because the British and French could fight here side by side. Now the French had few divisions to spare. Originally there were to have been forty French divisions and twenty-five British. This was changed to equality – twenty-five divisions each. Later, as the drain of Verdun went on, the French share was cut down to five divisions; and Foch, their commander, was of all men the most sceptical about the offensive. Moreover, the Somme was peculiarly unsuited as an object of attack. The Germans everywhere occupied the crests of the hills; the attackers had to fight their way upwards against a concealed enemy. There had been no previous fighting here on a serious scale, and the German defences had been for long neglected. But the British High Command, unlike the French and the Germans, believed in keeping their men on their toes by constant activity. These raids, which had no strategical purpose, not only wasted lives. They also provoked the Germans into strengthening their defences. Thus the British virtually fortified against themselves the position which they were planning to attack. By the summer of 1916, the German front line was heavily covered by barbed wire. Behind it was a second line, equally strong. The chalk made digging easy: and the Germans had dug-outs forty feet deep, complete with every modern convenience, which made them secure from the heaviest bombardment. It seems inconceivable that any army in the world could have forced such a line.

The British army had plenty of heavy artillery – or so it supposed before the battle started; in practice supplies of shell often ran out. The British infantry had enthusiasm, and not much else. These were the men who had answered Kitchener's call; hardly any were conscripts. They had received hasty and rudimentary training. They could not shoot accurately. They could not operate in scattered bodies. They had been taught only to go forward in a straight line. They had been instructed to rely mainly on the bayonet. When it came to real war, the British infantry of the Somme never saw those whom they were fighting; and the bayonet was used only to kill men who had already surrendered. The junior officers were also recruits, recently trained. They, too, had enthusiasm and little else. They had been taught to expose themselves recklessly – hence officer casualties were often six times greater than those of other ranks. They had also been taught to obey unquestioningly and never to show initiative. This great army of volunteers was the most rigid army of the Great War; the army, too, of harshest discipline and the most severe punishments. Nothing had been

98. British soldiers man a captured German trench on the Somme.

134

learnt from previous failures except how to repeat them on a larger scale. There was the same unreasoning faith in the offensive as had brought the French to disaster even in August 1914. Haig had one flicker of sense. He suggested that small scouting parties should be sent forward after the bombardment to make sure that the enemy defences had been obliterated. Rawlinson rejected this idea as beyond the competence of his men. Haig also laid down the attack should be broken off if it did not succeed at once. This idea, too, was not observed. Haig himself never doubted. He was confident that the cavalry would be sweeping through open country to Bapaume on the first afternoon.

The battle of the Somme was opened by five days of heavy bombardment on an eighteen-mile front. This was intended to destroy the enemy wire and front line. Instead it pitted the ground so heavily with shell craters as to make orderly advance impossible. Moreover the craters gave the Germans fresh cover for their machine guns even when their trenches were destroyed. Rawlinson proposed to attack at dawn or even before it. The French on the right wished to see the full effects of their artillery fire, and insisted on attacking in daylight. Rawlinson agreed, and fixed the attack for 7.30 a.m. When it came to the day, the French delayed another two hours, and thus took the

99. British cavalry wait for the breakthrough.

100. The artistry of war: gunfire at night.

101. The rewards of victory: British troops at the Somme.

Germans by surprise, achieving the one success of that calamitous day. On 1 July, thirteen British divisions went forward together. The men threaded their way through the British wire; then formed into a solid line, and sought to advance. Though their one chance was speed, they were weighed down by 66 lb. of equipment, and often much more – field telephones, carrier pigeons, picks and shovels. There was no way of calling for artillery assistance. The barrage automatically lifted at the moment of attack, and moved on to the second German line whether the first had been destroyed or not. Nor was there any means of concentrating on weak points and leaving the strong ones alone. The British line had to advance uniformly, or not at all. As the British struggled across No Man's Land, the Germans had plenty of time to emerge from their dug-outs and to man their machine guns. The bullets ran across the front in a steady spray. The first British line faltered and fell, a second followed it, a third, and then a fourth, all to no avail. By the early afternoon the survivors were back in their trenches, except for a small gain in the southern sector.

On 1 July the British sustained 60,000 casualties, 20,000 of them killed – the heaviest loss ever suffered in a single day by a British army or by any army in the First World War. The

102. British troops cross the canal bridge. But where is the canal?

103. The Somme: after the battle.

104. *British transport at the Somme.*

French had achieved their objectives with less loss to themselves than to the enemy; they could have gone forward further if it had not been for fear of endangering their left flank where it joined with the British. What now? The generals from Haig downwards had boasted of success too much to face the thought of breaking off. They concealed the truth even from themselves. In the words of the official history, 'captures of prisoners, but not the heavy casualties, were regularly reported'. Rawlinson did not attempt to exploit the few points of success, particularly with the French. Instead he ordered more uniform attacks all along the line; and each day the same tragic story was repeated on a diminishing scale. Yet reward was still waiting for the simplest surprise. Rawlinson decided to try a night attack, and extracted permission from Haig, after long argument. On 14 July some twenty thousand men attacked at 3.25 a.m. after only five minutes' bombardment. The Germans, who had thought their night's rest secure, were caught asleep. Five miles of their second line was overrun. Now came the great set piece of which all British generals dreamt: the cavalry were to go through. Three divisions were in readiness. They took a long time coming, held up in the mud and craters of the battlefield. At seven in the evening, the British infantry saw a sight unique

105. One of the first tanks in difficulty.

on the Western Front; cavalry riding into action through the waving corn with bugles blowing and lances glittering. The glorious vision crumbled into slaughter as the German machine guns opened fire.

After this, the fighting dragged stubbornly forward to no purpose. On 15 September Haig decided to use the few tanks available, despite the urging of the experts to wait until they could be used in real weight. The tanks were untried. Some broke down. A few penetrated the German lines, but with no infantry to follow. The surprise of a really heavy attack by tanks was lost. The Germans, however, did not heed the warning. By now the rains of autumn were falling. The front churned into mud. There was a last attack on 13 November. Then the battle, if such it can be called, came to its dismal end. There had been no breakthrough. The front had advanced here and there about five miles. Beyond this the German line was as strong as ever. The British lost some 420,000 casualties: the French nearly 200,000. The Germans probably lost about 450,000; and would have lost less if it had not been for the order of Falkenhayn, rivalling Haig's in obstinacy, that every yard of lost trench must be retaken by counter-attacks. Many years later, the editor of the British official history performed a conjuring trick on the German figures, and blew them up to 650,000, thus making out against all experience that the attackers suffered less than the defence. There is no need to take those figures seriously.

Strategically, the battle of the Somme was an unredeemed defeat. It is supposed to have worn down the spirit of the German army. So no doubt it did, though not to the point of crippling that army as a fighting machine. The German spirit was not the only one to suffer. The British were worn down also. Idealism perished on the Somme. The enthusiastic volunteers were enthusiastic no longer. They had lost faith in their cause, in their leaders, in everything except loyalty to their fighting comrades. The war ceased to have a purpose. It went on for its own sake, as a contest in endurance. Rupert Brooke had symbolized the British soldier at the beginning of the war. Now his place was taken by Old Bill, a veteran of 1915, who crouched in a shell crater for want of 'a better 'ole to go to'. The Somme set the picture by which future generations saw the First World War: brave helpless soldiers; blundering obstinate generals; nothing achieved. After the Somme men decided that the war would go on for ever.

Such was the military record of 1916. War became a great
industry. Guns and the shells to feed them were produced in
unimaginable number. Far from restoring the war of movement, they made movement impossible. The bodies of men were
sacrificed to no purpose. Only disenchantment was the result.
The great guns were also heard at sea, though here again with
no decisive effect. 1916 saw the only occasion when two modern
battle fleets engaged in European waters. At the beginning of
the year there was a change in Germany's naval command.
Scheer, who took over the High Seas Fleet, was eager for action.
He recognized that the British fleet was superior, but he hoped
to entice their ships into isolated actions and thus wear down
British strength until something like equality was achieved.
Hence he pushed provocatively into the North Sea. The British
could follow every German move. Early in the war, the body
of a dead German naval officer was found by the Russians in
the Baltic. On it was a copy of the German code book. The
Russians passed this to the British – a rare act of Allied cooperation. Henceforth the British could decipher every German
wireless message. The great day came on 31 May. Scheer set
his trap. Admiral Hipper, with the battle cruisers, was to go
ahead, and to lure British ships on to the main fleet. The British
heard the warning. From Scapa Flow, Jellicoe steamed south

The war at sea.

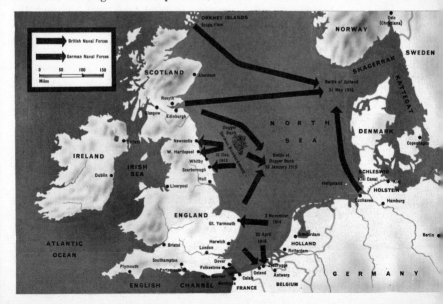

106. He could have lost the war in an afternoon: Jellicoe on his flagship, the Iron Duke.

with the Grand Fleet to take the Germans in their own trap. There had never been such an array of naval might. The British had twenty-eight dreadnoughts and nine battle cruisers; the Germans sixteen dreadnoughts and five battle cruisers. In all 250 vessels were present, and no less than twenty-five admirals. Curiously little came of it all.

At first everything went according to plan. Beatty, commanding the British battle cruisers, engaged Hipper in the early afternoon. Though two British ships were sunk, Beatty pushed on towards the main German fleet. Scheer thought that his great chance had come. Beatty turned away, apparently in flight. For two hours Scheer pursued him. At 6.15 p.m. the main British fleet appeared on the horizon, and deployed into line, though in such a way as to deploy away from the enemy. Scheer saw the trap almost before the great guns began to fire. He, too, turned away, soon after 6.30. Jellicoe did not attempt to pursue. He had laid down the firm doctrine that it was more important to preserve British ships than to sink German; and he now believed that pursuit would bring his ships on to German mines or German submarines. In fact, the Germans had none of either on the scene of battle. However, rightly or wrongly, Jellicoe turned away. The battle seemed over. Half an hour later Scheer's ships suddenly reappeared, slap in the centre of the British line. No one knows why: probably Scheer hoped to pass across their rear. The battle was renewed for some fifteen minutes. Then Scheer turned away once more, and Jellicoe also. The British were now between the Germans and their way home. But contact had been lost. Jellicoe could only guess at the German route, and he guessed the wrong one. In London the Admiralty deciphered yet another German message; and informed Jellicoe of Scheer's route. Jellicoe took no notice; perhaps he distrusted such new-fangled inventions as wireless. Scheer slipped past the British rear, and got safely home. Jellicoe found himself on an empty sea, and went home in his turn. The battle of Jutland was over.

Who won? The British lost more ships – three battle cruisers, three cruisers, eight destroyers as against one German battleship, one battle cruiser, four light cruisers, and five destroyers. British gunnery was inferior to the German, and their armour defective – at least one battle cruiser blew up from a spark passing down the hoist to the ammunition. But, at the decisive moment, the German fleet fled from the British; and, in Jellicoe's eyes, this was all that mattered. He did not suppose that he could win the war by destroying the German fleet; he

107. Admiral von Scheer (right).

108. *German fleet in action.*

thought that he might lose it if he did not preserve his own. Many people in England did not accept this doctrine; and in the following year Jellicoe was replaced by the more aggressive Beatty. Once in command, Beatty, too, became cautious. He, too, recognized that the Grand Fleet must remain in harbour unless the Germans came out. The Germans made two tentative appearances, and then withdrew in good time. The two fleets cancelled out. The British still operated their distant blockade. They still drew supplies from all over the world. The real danger to Great Britain did not come from any German belief that they had won the battle of Jutland. It came from their appreciation that they had lost it, or at any rate that they could not gain from fighting another battle of the same kind. German shipyards were switched from building surface ships to building submarines. German sailors were taken off their ships and trained for submarine warfare. German admirals and German generals alike drew the lesson from their failures of 1916 that an unrestricted submarine campaign was Germany's decisive card. Strategically this was the legacy of the year.

The civilian populations felt that the war was drawing nearer to them. The casualty lists were no longer those of remote heroes. They contained the names of everyone's friends and

relatives. In this year, too, came the only lasting mark which
the First World War made on men's lives: Daylight Saving as
it was called then, Summer Time as we call it now. The war did
better than Joshua. It made the sun change its place in the
heavens, or at any rate made men pretend that it had done so.
Yet men were still reluctant to tamper with free choice and the
workings of 'economic law'. Though even the British finally
swallowed compulsory military service for all, whether married
or unmarried, in May 1916, there was still little direction of
labour for civil purposes in any country. Prices were going up
everywhere, and little was done about it. There had been stable
prices and stable currencies as long as anyone living could
remember. Now men could not understand what was happening. They blamed human wickedness – the greed of profiteers
or of trade unions – instead of appreciating that when governments paid their bills with paper money, not from taxation,
inflation would follow. Bread was rationed in some countries.
Otherwise there was 'rationing by the purse'. Food prices were
simply allowed to rise. The Germans had already started the
story that their food shortage was due to the British 'hunger
blockade'. Yet Germany had not imported food before the war.
The truth is that the Germans starved themselves. They took

*109. Women of
Berlin scavenge
for food.*

millions of men from the land for the armies. High prices encouraged the peasants to send their pigs and cattle to market. Then supplies ran short. 1916 saw a bad harvest, followed by a bitter winter. Turnips became the staple diet. The 'turnip winter' remained, for many, the sharpest memory of the war. The British escaped this hardship. Bread was never rationed in Great Britain. The worst the British experienced was the adulteration of wheat by other flour – at first rye and maize, later potato. This produced an imaginary, though painful, war-indigestion.

Despite these hardships, there was as yet little active discontent. In most countries, though not in Russia, trade union leaders cooperated with the governments to get the smooth running of industry; and the workers were kept quiet by increases of wages. A few Socialists from the belligerent countries met in Switzerland, and called on the working classes everywhere to end the war. This was not extreme enough for Lenin, who wanted to turn the Imperialist war into a civil war. The workers took no notice of either appeal. Nor did the grievances of oppressed nationalities cause much trouble. Czech units in the Austro-Hungarian army often deserted at a suitable moment on the Russian front; this was more from loyalty to the Good Soldier Schweik than from any national ideal. In February a few Czech exiles in Paris set up a National Council, which claimed independence for their people. The Allies took little notice of this Council, the Government of Austria-Hungary still less, the Czechs at home least of all. Professor Masaryk, spokesman of the Czech nation, thought himself in luck's way when Asquith agreed to take the chair for him at an academic lecture in King's College, London. At the last moment Asquith cried off. The freedom of small peoples had not got far.

One small people struck a blow for their freedom in 1916 – the only national rebellion which occurred anywhere at any time in the war. Before the war Ireland had been near to civil conflict: the majority of Irishmen demanding Home Rule, a minority in Ulster preparing to resist it even at the price of civil war. Virtually all Irishmen rallied enthusiastically to the cause of Belgium. Home Rule was suspended for the duration. Irishmen, both Roman Catholic and Protestant, enlisted in the British army. The Ulster Volunteers, who had been planning rebellion with German assistance, were taken over as official units. The Irish Volunteers, who had merely claimed their legal rights, were ignored. The Red Hand of Ulster became an official military symbol; the Irish Harp remained unrecognized. Some of the Irish Volunteers resented this. About ten thousand (out of 140,000) broke away, and prepared in their turn for rebellion. They, too, like the Ulster Volunteers before them, sought German assistance. Sir Roger Casement, one-time British consul, went first to the United States, then to Germany. He tried to enlist Irish prisoners of war in an Irish Legion. He had little success. He urged the Germans to land arms and men in Ireland as assistance for a rising. The German officials, conservative and respectable, did not like such subversive ideas; they also thought invasion of Ireland impracticable. However, a rising was fixed for Easter 1916. At the last moment Casement realized that the Germans were cheating him: they had no intention of sending any real support. He left Germany, and landed in Ireland from a German submarine in order to warn his associates against attempting a rebellion. He failed to give the warning. He wandered alone on a desolate shore, and was arrested within a few hours of landing.

In Ireland, too, there had been doubts. John Macneill, Chief of Staff of the Irish Volunteers, first resigned his post; then thought better of it, and issued orders that the rising was

110. Irish heroines run German guns to Ireland.

cancelled. Most of the ten thousand went home. In Dublin a few leaders determined to go on. They managed to bring out altogether about two thousand men. They failed to seize Dublin Castle, the centre of administration, though it had a garrison of only twenty men. On Easter Monday 1916, they set up headquarters at the central post office, and proclaimed the Irish Republic. Five days of fighting followed. British guns damaged the shopping streets of central Dublin. On the Friday after Easter the Irish surrendered. The rebels had been un-popular in their own country, where most people had friends or relations serving with the British army. The British Government turned the rebels into heroes by a policy of bloodshed. All the seven men who signed the Proclamation of the Republic were shot – one of them badly wounded, being carried out to death in a chair; all the Volunteer commandants were shot except one – de Valera, who was technically not of British nationality. Casement was taken to London and charged with high treason; his prosecutor, F. E. Smith, had been a leading advocate of high treason in Ulster two years before. Casement was found guilty and sentenced to death. There were murmurs of a demand for reprieve. To silence these, the British Government circulated passages, perhaps genuine, from Casement's

112. British rule triumphs in Ireland.

113. A republican barricade in Dublin.

diary, showing that he was homosexual. The demand was silenced. Casement was hanged. Meanwhile, some thousands of Irishmen were sent, without trial, to concentration camps in England. This was an ironic comment on the British claim to be fighting for the liberty of small nations. However, it caused no twinge of conscience. The British Government, like every other, still paraded unshakeable confidence in the righteousness of their cause, and, a more urgent matter, in the certainty of victory.

Behind the scenes, generals and politicians regarded each other with increasing suspicion. Nearly all believed that the war would go better if only there were a few changes at the top. The first to go was Kitchener. He had already lost all real influence over affairs. He was pushed into visiting Russia. On 5 June the cruiser *Hampshire*, which was taking him, struck a mine off the Orkneys. Kitchener and nearly all the crew were drowned. It was a sad and yet a noble end. In earlier wars, and in the Second World War, generals, even marshals, also ran risks and died in action. In the First World War they led comfortable lives. All except Kitchener. He was the only outstanding military figure on either side who came to a violent end. Asquith announced that a memorial would be erected to him

after the war. When the war ended, Kitchener was forgotten;
no memorial was built. No one took his place as a popular
symbol. Lloyd George succeeded him at the War Office, only
to discover that the arrangements made to deprive Kitchener
of power operated also against himself. Robertson was still
supreme director of strategy; and this reinforced Lloyd George's
determination to force a change at the top.

Falkenhayn was the next to topple. Though a competent
military leader, rather more competent than most others, he
lacked glamour. Someone with more prestige was needed to
cloak the comparative failures at Verdun and on the Somme.
The final blow came when Rumania, tempted by the apparent
success of Brusilov's offensive, entered the war against Germany
on 27 August. Falkenhayn could hardly be blamed for the fact
that the Allies had bribed Rumania into the war by lavish
promises of Hungarian territory. But German opinion had to
be given some dramatic encouragement. The symbol was ready
to hand: Hindenburg, the wooden titan. He was hastily summoned to imperial headquarters, and made Chief of the General
Staff, with Ludendorff at his side as the directing mind. Falkenhayn was put in charge of the Rumanian campaign, and conducted it so successfully that before the end of the year

114. The
Hindenburg line.

115. Falkenhayn (third from right) *is victorious in Rumania.*

practically all Rumania was overrun by the German armies. Before this happened, British agents managed to destroy most of the Rumanian oil wells; and Germany drew little oil from Rumania for the rest of the war.

Hindenburg, or rather Ludendorff speaking through Hindenburg, had kept up a running stream of criticism against Falkenhayn from the remote fastness of the Eastern Front. Ludendorff was confident that the victors of Tannenberg could win the war in the west if placed in supreme command. Once there, Ludendorff appreciated Falkenhayn's difficulties for the first time. The food shortage weighed with him heavily; so, too, did the virtual collapse of the Austro-Hungarian army. Without delay, he increased his own power. He called on Groener, a general who got on well with trade union leaders, to set up the *Kriegsamt*. This body organized the civilian manpower of Germany for war. In theory it could conscribe all male labour between eighteen and sixty. In practice Groener relied on the appeal of higher wages. Ludendorff also secured the subordination of the Austro-Hungarian army to German headquarters. From this moment, the Habsburg Monarchy ceased to be an independent country from a military point of view.

None of this helped Ludendorff on the Western Front. He used Hindenburg's prestige immediately to cover a change of strategy which Falkenhayn had not dared to risk. Ludendorff stopped the fight for every yard of trench. Henceforth the German troops gave ground, and so reduced their losses. Ludendorff went further; he resolved to simplify the German line. Every village and field in the west had sentimental value for the French; they had none for the Germans. Throughout the winter, the German services in the rear laboured to prepare a new 'Hindenburg line', systematically chosen for its advantages instead of imposed by accident. The work went on securely, remote from Allied interference. Dug-outs were constructed and equipped; concrete positions were built for machine guns; a network of light railways was laid down almost up to the front line. In this way, Ludendorff could look forward to a successful defence, conducted with fewer divisions. Nevertheless, with Russia still in the war and apparently unshaken, he had no hope for decisive victory. He could defend Germany, no more. Hence he, too, came back to the policy long preached by Falkenhayn and the admirals: unrestricted submarine warfare. He preached it with the additional force of Hindenburg's prestige.

Thus began the great conflict over German policy. Bethmann, the Chancellor, had lacked faith in decisive victory from the beginning. His intention all along had been to propose a compromise peace, but only when others – generals, admirals, and the German people – came round to agreeing with him that victory was impossible. He had actually backed the appointment of Hindenburg and Ludendorff, in the calculation that Hindenburg's prestige would make a compromise peace easier. The plan rebounded on him: the prestige was being used instead to enforce submarine warfare. Here, too, Bethmann had no faith; he was as sceptical of admirals as he had been of generals. Instead, he had acute fear that an unrestricted submarine campaign would bring the United States into the war; it would indeed break the deadlock, but on the wrong side. Bethmann could not simply use his authority as Chancellor. He had little to use. Like the civilian leaders in every country, Bethmann had deliberately built up the prestige of the generals in order to sustain popular enthusiasm for the war. Now this prestige was too strong for him. It was beyond Bethmann's power to forbid unrestricted submarine warfare. His only hope was to secure a peace satisfactory to Germany before the submarines began to operate. Yet the peace had to be as good as victory,

116. The Lord thanked once more: Field-Marshal Mackensen leaves church at Bucarest.

117. The smoke of burning oil at Constanza.

if it were to silence the admirals, who were promising that they could win decisive victory by bringing Great Britain to starvation.

There was a further difficulty. Even those who believed that decisive victory was impossible for themselves – and they existed in every belligerent country – also believed that it was impossible for the enemy. Deadlock, they argued, pointed to a compromise peace; and this meant a return to the *status quo*, accompanied by mutual concessions. But what was the *status quo?* The Allies regarded it as the situation of June 1914, before the war started; in German eyes, it was the situation of autumn 1916. The Allies took the pre-war frontiers as the starting point; the Germans took the existing lines of trenches. In the Allied view, it would be a generous compromise if the German armies were allowed to go home without being punished for their aggression and after paying for the damage they had caused. The German idea of compromise was that they should keep some of their wartime conquests and be paid for surrendering the rest. Deadlock, which was expected to promote compromise, really worked against it. Neither side would accept the version of compromise put forward by the other unless defeat threatened; in that case the victor need not think of compromise.

The situation might have been different if any belligerent government had felt itself threatened by domestic discontent and revolution. Strangely enough, at this time none did, except that of Austria-Hungary; and it was firmly shackled under German control. On the contrary, governments, and still more individual statesmen, feared for their position only if they failed to fulfil their promises of decisive victory; and even those who no longer believed these promises had to go on making them.

Germany's best hope was not of a general peace. It was to detach some single Ally, and thus have more chance of victory over the others. Falkenhayn had tried to do this with France. He had failed. Bethmann tried it with Russia, by means of negotiation. This seemed more promising. The Tsar and his reactionary ministers had no interest in a decisive victory for the Western Powers, still less in a war to make the world safe for democracy. Germany, on an abstract calculation, had little to gain from acquiring land in the east – little, at any rate, compared to the industrial rewards which she hoped to gather in the west. Bethmann tentatively offered to withdraw behind the German frontiers of 1914. The Tsar's government were on the point of responding. Then Ludendorff intervened. He refused to renounce the eastern conquests which he and Hindenburg had made. If he did, what would happen to Hindenburg's prestige? Besides, he was obsessed with finding more manpower for future campaigns; and believed that the Poles would enlist enthusiastically on the German side if they were promised independence. In November 1916 the promise was made. It ended all chance of a compromise peace with Russia. No reward followed. The Poles had no faith in Germany's promise. Only 1,400 enlisted, instead of the fifteen divisions which Ludendorff had expected. In this odd way, German soldiers on the Eastern Front had to go on fighting for the sake of Polish independence – or rather for the sake of a promise of independence in which neither Poles nor Germans believed.

Bethmann saw unrestricted submarine warfare, and with it American intervention, drawing even nearer. His last resort was to propose peace negotiations, not in the hope of any result, but to keep America neutral. On 12 December, the German Government issued a Peace Note, making a vague offer of negotiations with the Allies. No German terms were stated. Bethmann meant to demand the French iron-ore fields in Lorraine, economic control over Belgium, the Belgian Congo, and a kingdom of Poland under German protection – to say nothing of Balkan gains for Austria-Hungary. The German generals meant to demand a good deal more. They argued that Germany had been attacked by France and Russia in 1914; and that only gains on a great scale could secure her from similar attacks in the future. However the German demands were never made public. The Allies rejected the offer of negotiations out of hand.

Yet behind the scenes there was considerable talk of peace in some Allied countries also during the autumn of 1916. There was a rather different emphasis. In Germany many leading figures acknowledged that decisive victory was impossible, and therefore asked: what would be tolerable terms for ending the war? On the Allied side, men still stuck at the first question: is victory impossible? Unlike Ludendorff, the Allied generals still returned a confident answer. Haig promised final victory in Flanders some time in 1917. Robertson was astonished that the question should even be asked. Joffre had undiminished faith in attrition, though now he expected the British to do most of the killing and to bear most of the sacrifice. But Joffre's days of power were drawing to a close. In the French Chamber, deputies denounced the long list of casualties and Joffre's indifference to it. Briand, the Prime Minister, resolved to get rid of Joffre in order to save himself. Chance produced a strange successor. Late in October, when fighting seemed over, General Nivelle, who was in local command at Verdun, took the Germans by surprise, and recaptured practically all that the French had lost earlier in the year, with very light casualties. He became a national hero overnight. Nivelle announced that he had discovered the secret of victory, though he did not reveal what this secret was. The temptation was irresistible. Joffre was pushed upstairs. He became a Marshal of France, and lost all influence on the war. Nivelle took his place as supreme commander on the Western Front. Briand had intended a smart stroke. He got rid of Joffre without fuss. But he had saddled himself instead with a new commander even more set on decisive victory, though other French generals insisted, almost without exception, that the French armies were incapable of a fresh offensive. Thus Briand was in no position even to air the question of a compromise peace.

In Great Britain there was more serious discussion. Some civilian ministers refused to share the conviction of the generals. The Liberals, Runciman and McKenna, believed that Great Britain was near to economic collapse. Lord Lansdowne,

118. He thought he had the secret of victory: General Nivelle.

Conservative leader in the House of Lords, argued more sweepingly that the fabric of European civilization could not survive more years of war. None of them dared say these things in public. Lloyd George, on the other hand, raised an enthusiastic response when he called for 'the knock-out blow'. The British were fighting for great moral principles, or so most of them believed; and these principles could be asserted only by the full defeat of Germany, not by a compromise peace. Lloyd George did not believe that the war could be won if things went on as they were at present – no coordination between the Allies, no ruthless marshalling of national resources for war. Attending an Allied conference at Paris in November, he said gloomily to his companion, Maurice Hankey: 'We are going to lose this war.' Lloyd George determined to secure a more energetic conduct of the war. Bonar Law, the Conservative leader, seconded him. Lloyd George's original intention was to demand direction of the war for himself, with Asquith remaining Prime Minister as a figurehead. Asquith at first agreed, then changed his mind. He regarded himself as 'the indispensable man'; and therefore supposed that, by breaking up his government, he could re-form it either without Lloyd George or with a Lloyd George thoroughly tamed.

The calculation did not work. Once out, Asquith could not get back. Ordinary M.P.s, both Conservative and Liberal, also wanted 'a more energetic conduct of the war', they did not mind from whom; and they recognized that they were more likely to get it from Lloyd George. Bonar Law, cajoled by Beaverbrook, brought in the Conservatives. Christopher Addison 'whipped' 120 Liberals. Lloyd George pulled off a particularly effective stroke when he won the backing of the Labour party – small in the House of Commons, but bringing with it the cooperation of the trade unions in the factories. On 5 December 1916 Lloyd George became Prime Minister. He set up a War Cabinet of five – himself, Bonar Law, Milner, Curzon, and Henderson; men free from departmental ties who would concentrate on winning the war. He called in business-men and trade union leaders as ministers. Asquith and the former Liberal ministers withdrew into Opposition – the first official Opposition since May 1915. They were still committed to supporting the war. After all, Asquith and Grey had led the country into war; Lloyd George had opposed it till the last moment. All the same, the Liberals were out to make things difficult for Lloyd George if they could. His strength came not only from the backbenchers in Parliament. It came still more

119. Success is pleasant: Lloyd George and Churchill on the march to the top.

from the British people. He was the one popular figure, the man who could win the war – as indeed he did.

Lloyd George's rise to supreme power ended, by implication, the rumbling talk in London of a compromise peace. This was not its direct intention. No one revealed that any such talk was going on. But by promising to run the war better, Lloyd George committed himself to the doctrine that it could be won, and should be won. Discussion of a compromise peace was automatically ruled off the agenda. Bethmann's Peace Note of 12 December came at an opportune moment for Lloyd George. When he first met the House as Prime Minister, he spent his time denouncing Bethmann, and thus avoided any awkward explanation of why he had overthrown Asquith, while Asquith on his side could not criticize Lloyd George without seeming to endorse Bethmann. The new government flourished under the impression that it had been formed to ward off Bethmann's wiles.

Peace talk did not altogether vanish beneath the horizon. From the first day of the war President Wilson, over in the United States, had looked forward to the time when he would appear as mediator, posed impartially between the contending parties. He wanted a 'peace without victory', which would then be guaranteed by the United States. Hence he had clung to neutrality despite the provocation of the British blockade and the worse provocation of the German submarines. After the sinking of the *Lusitania* the only menacing sound heard from Washington was the rattle of the President's typewriter. Then the rattle had worked. The Germans had agreed to observe the rules of war at sea. By the autumn of 1916, Wilson, like Bethmann, saw unrestricted submarine warfare by the Germans again approaching. Now was his last chance to mediate. Wilson also hoped that the military deadlock was turning the belligerents towards compromise. But he was not free to act while the situation was still open. All his energies were diverted into the presidential campaign until he was re-elected, as 'the man who kept us out of the war', in November 1916. There were further delays of drafting. Only on 18 December did Wilson invite the belligerents to state their respective aims; perhaps 'they would not prove irreconcilable'. The invitation came too late. The elevation of Lloyd George in Great Britain, of Nivelle in France, to say nothing of Ludendorff's growing authority in Germany, had turned all the main belligerents against compromise. Both sides were indignant at Wilson's suggestion that there was little to choose between them. The Germans simply refused Wilson's invitation with the excuse that they had already offered to negotiate. Really they recognized that their terms would outrage Wilson, as indeed they did when he learnt them later, and so kept quiet about them.

The Germans were only concerned to keep the United States neutral. The Allies however wished to win America to their side. They had to give a more positive reply – to define the moral superiority, which they really felt, in such a way as to satisfy American idealism. The British and French governments had hastily to discover what they were fighting for. They came out with an answer on 10 January 1917. It was easy to demand the evacuation of all territory occupied by Germany, and its restoration at German expense – Belgium, Serbia, Rumania, western Russia, and northern France. Beyond this they had no idea what to do with Germany except to defeat her. They therefore spoke vaguely of 'full security and international settlements such as to guarantee land and sea frontiers against unjustified attack'. This was not enough as an appeal to American sentiment. The Allies had also to display some great principle. They found it in 'national self-determination'. This did not affect Germany, except in regard to Alsace and Lorraine; for the Allies dared not mention Poland so long as the Tsar was their ally. Hence the principle hit only Austria-Hungary and the Ottoman Empire. The Allies demanded 'the liberation of the Italians, as also of the Slavs, Rumanians, and Czechoslovaks from foreign domination' and 'the freeing of the populations subject to the bloody tyranny of the Turks'. This was an extraordinary outcome. The Allies were fighting Germany. They had no quarrel with Austria-Hungary and Turkey except as Germany's allies. Yet here they were, laying down the dismemberment of Austria-Hungary and the Turkish Empire as their one practical war-aim. No one had contemplated such an aim when war started in 1914. The man in the street had not been consulted, and was bewildered to be told that this was what he was fighting for. War-aims had formerly been chosen in order to make victory easier. This demand did the opposite. It became more difficult to detach Austria-Hungary, or even Turkey, from the German side, though doing so would obviously help towards victory. The idealistic war-aim no doubt affected American opinion; but the United States were brought into the war by the German submarines, not by a shift of opinion.

At any rate, the Allied note of 10 January 1917, itself a

120. A solitary voice against war: Karl Liebknecht speaks in Berlin.

postscript, ended all talk of a compromise peace. In later years, men often looked back to the autumn of 1916, and lamented the lost chance of ending the war before old Europe perished. The historian does not deal in these 'might-have-beens'. At most, he can suggest why the chance was not taken. In every country, some men of great influence were still confident that the war could be won. The German admirals promised to bring Great Britain to her knees within six weeks, if their U-boats were allowed to sink at sight; Ludendorff backed them. In England Lloyd George had supreme faith in his capacity to organize the country for war; Haig and Robertson were certain of victory, though they did not know how. The French Government were dazzled by Nivelle and his mighty secret. Of course, there was in them all an element of wishful thinking. The generals and statesmen had promised victory so often that they came to believe their own promises. Besides, talk of victory brought popular applause. Those who advocated a compromise peace had their meetings broken up, and their newspapers burnt. Karl Liebknecht was imprisoned in Germany; Bertrand Russell in England. No doubt the men in the trenches would have been delighted if they had been told that the war was ended, on whatever terms. Yet a great outcry would have followed if it had then been revealed that the war had not ended with victory. After all, there was plenty of outcry in Great Britain and France in 1918 against a 'soft' peace, even after a decisive victory. It was necessary to rouse public opinion in order to fight the war; and this opinion then made it essential to keep the war going. In every country the rulers feared the consequences of ending the war more than they feared the consequences of continuing it.

Things might have been different if there had been solid grounds for a general compromise. There were not. At bottom both sides were fighting for the same object: increased security so that there would never be another war. They translated this object into conflicting terms. The Germans demanded territorial gains which would make impossible another attack by France and Russia. The Allies saw in these gains demands which would make another attack by Germany only too likely. On their side, the Allies sought security by a convincing demonstration that aggression – meaning German aggression – did not pay; and this could be shown only by a decisive defeat of the German army. According to the Allies, the future could be made secure only by an assertion of moral principles, principles which in German eyes meant the subordination of Germany to the other Powers of Europe. The divergence can be defined in narrower terms. The British, unless within sight of complete defeat, would be satisfied with nothing less than the evacuation and restoration of Belgium. Equally the Germans, unless within sight of complete defeat, would not leave Belgium without rich compensation for the country which they had so easily overrun. To a detached view, the military deadlock ought to have produced a willingness to compromise. It did the opposite. Both sides asked: 'Why should we compromise when we cannot be defeated?' Only victory seemed to promise security; and men went on fighting the war in order to make certain that there would never be another.

121. Eton boys do their bit.

1917

If Napoleon had come back to life at the beginning of 1917, he would have found nothing which surprised him or which, at any rate, he could not understand: much the same European Powers as in his day fighting much the same sort of war on a rather larger scale. He would have recognized tsars and emperors and even liberal politicians. But suppose he put off his return a few months and came back at the end of the year, then he would have been bewildered. At one end of Europe was Bolshevism, an entirely new system of thought and government. At the other end of Europe the United States, a power unconnected with Europe, was beginning to intervene on a scale which would eclipse all the traditional Great Powers put together. In 1917 European history, in the old sense, came to an end. World history began. It was the year of Lenin and Woodrow Wilson, both of whom repudiated the traditional standards of political behaviour. Both preached Utopia, Heaven on Earth. It was the moment of birth for our contemporary world; the dramatic moment of modern man's existence.

New men and new methods set the theme of 1917 from the start. At the outset, however, the theme was no more than a variation on the accepted pattern. The new men of 1917 were expected to be Lloyd George and Ludendorff. Both men promised a full and final victory, a knock-out blow. Both were anxious to use new methods in order to achieve this full and final victory. The war became clearly an Anglo-German duel, with their respective allies keeping up as best they could. Of course the man in the trenches or the housewife queueing for bread did not notice any change. For them the war dragged on its weary way as before. Yet there was a change: less enthusiasm and more organization, or an attempt at it. Both Ludendorff and Lloyd George subordinated everything to the needs of war. British shipping was put under government control. Labour was directed to munition factories. County agricultural committees supervised the growing of food. Lloyd George believed that the war could be won only if all the resources of the Allies were put in a common pool under common control. At his prompting, a great Allied Conference met in Rome. Nothing came of it except highsounding talk.

Lloyd George had a more practical aim when he summoned

the Rome Conference: he wanted to shift the main theatre of war from the Western Front in France. He did not believe that anything could be achieved by more slaughter there. Above all he had no faith in Haig, the British Commander-in-Chief. He thought other British generals just as bad. Besides, he feared that his own supporters in the House of Commons would turn against him if he dismissed Haig. What was more, Haig enjoyed the protection of King George V who made him a field marshal at this time as a gesture of defiance against Lloyd George. At Rome, Lloyd George proposed that the great effort of the year should be made on the Italian front. Cadorna, the Italian Commander-in-Chief, turned down the proposal. He was frightened of his French and British colleagues; perhaps still more frightened of the responsibility for running a decisive campaign. Lloyd George left Rome bitter and disappointed. He was committed to the knock-out blow; yet striking this blow on the Italian front had been rejected by all concerned. His very enthusiasm for victory chained him to the Western Front after all.

Nivelle's plan for a great offensive was already on the agenda of the War Cabinet. Lloyd George did not like it. At the Rome Conference he tried to kill it, and failed. Nivelle came to London in order to urge it afresh. Haig came also, equally urgent for an offensive in France. Nivelle was handsome, young, energetic. Unlike most generals, he expressed his thoughts in clear, well-formed sentences; he spoke good English. Gradually, Lloyd George saw a way out. He had confidence in French generals, though none in British. There should indeed be an offensive on the Western Front, but solely under Nivelle. Haig would at last be brought under control. In this strange way, Lloyd George, opponent of the Western Front, became for a brief period its strongest advocate. Nivelle was secretly told to prepare a scheme for giving him command over the British army as well as his own. The War Cabinet approved the scheme without consulting Sir William Robertson, the Chief of Staff. He was only told that nothing important was to be discussed and that he need not attend the meeting. Haig, suspecting nothing, meanwhile pushed on his own preparations for a new offensive, which might or might not fit in with Nivelle's plan.

On 26 February an Anglo-French conference was held at Calais, ostensibly to discuss improvements in the railways to the British front. Lloyd George innocently asked Nivelle to suggest means of cooperation. Nivelle produced the scheme for putting Haig under his orders which the War Cabinet had

already approved. Robertson exploded: 'Get 'Aig.' The two generals protested fiercely against putting the British army under the command of a foreigner. Haig objected even more because Nivelle was technically his junior. The scheme was watered down. It was to operate only during the coming offensive, and Haig was allowed to appeal to London if he thought his army endangered. Essentially Lloyd George got his way. There was a single command in France, and it was not the command of Sir Douglas Haig. In all the rush and quarrel, everyone missed the real objection that Nivelle was both commanding the French army and exercising supreme command at the same time. There were worse difficulties to come. Nivelle had 'formed a picture', as Napoleon warned generals not to do (though he sometimes did it himself). The Nivelle plan simply assumed that the Germans would behave in a certain way. They would remain where they were in the front line, wrapped in ignorance and taking no precautions. Nivelle selected a spot where he wanted the Germans to be weak, and then insisted that they were. Here the French armies would break through: 'Laon in twenty-four hours and then the pursuit.'

The Germans did not conform to Nivelle's requirements. Their new fortified line was ready by the beginning of March.

123. *No longer too proud to fight: President Wilson announces to Congress the breaking off of relations with Germany.*

They quietly withdrew to it. The salient which Nivelle had proposed to 'pinch out' disappeared. The Germans were now in a stronger position, which freed fifteen divisions for their reserve. They left a desolate area, sometimes fifty miles deep, in which everything had been systematically wrecked. Houses had been blown up, roads mined, wells poisoned. The British and French had to push forward over this obstacle, construct a new line, and then provide roads and railways to it. Still Nivelle was undismayed. His plan was to be followed exactly as laid down. By now Nivelle had lost his backer, Briand. Ribot, an old gentleman of eighty, had become Prime Minister. Painlevé, a distinguished mathematician, was Minister of War. These men had no faith in Nivelle. They questioned him, urged him to think again. Nivelle remained unshaken. Painlevé consulted other French generals. All foresaw failure. So did Haig and Robertson. In answer, Nivelle threatened to resign. Then, not only would the French public be indignant, the British army would no longer be under French orders. This silenced all criticism. Nivelle's plan was allowed to go forward. Thus, Lloyd George, distrusting his own generals, placed an unanswerable argument in the hands of a French general, who was even more distrusted by everyone except Lloyd George.

While these wrangles were going on, the face of the world changed so drastically as to make them both pointless and out of date. The Western Front was being eclipsed by events elsewhere, whether the British and French generals liked it or not. On 31 January the Germans took the fatal plunge. They announced the immediate introduction of unrestricted submarine warfare. All shipping, including neutral, would be sunk at sight in the war zone of the eastern Atlantic. On 2 February President Wilson broke off relations with Germany. He still hoped to avoid entering the war, and so be free to offer himself again as impartial mediator. The Germans wilfully destroyed his hope. Their submarines at once sank American ships. Zimmermann, the German Secretary of State, completed the process by a bright idea such as only a Foreign Office could conceive. He offered to help Mexico in a war for the recovery of New Mexico and other territory which the Americans had seized many years before. Of course, Germany had no means of providing help, and the Mexicans no intention of going to war. The offer was pure fantasy. The British Secret Service intercepted the telegram, and broke its code. They prompted the Americans to bribe a clerk in the German legation at Mexico

City. He revealed the text of the message. The Zimmermann telegram was published in the American papers. This gave the final push. On 6 April the United States declared war on Germany. Wilson lamented to the last. He said: 'It means that we shall lose our heads along with the rest and stop weighing right and wrong.' He spoke truly. The Americans had been the most reluctant to enter the war. Once in, they became the most ruthless and intolerant. Critics and doubters were persecuted. Since the security of America was not endangered, the Americans had to treat the war exclusively as a moral crusade. They insisted more strongly than anyone else that they were entirely in the right and the Germans entirely in the wrong. Yet Wilson, at any rate, had also doubts about the morality of the Allies. He refused to tie himself to them; and the United States remained throughout only an Associated Power.

German submarines forced the United States into the war. But it would be too simple to say that America fought solely for the freedom of the seas, still less of course for the sake of New Mexico. The United States were already committed to the Allied side. At first, the American Government had tried to remain strictly neutral. Banks were instructed not to give credit to the belligerents. Soon businessmen complained that

124. American troops practise against the Mexicans.

the chance of great profits was being lost. Large funds were extended to the Allies. Copper, cotton, wheat poured across the Atlantic. Factories worked overtime on British and French orders. The economy boomed. If the German submarines stopped this trade, there would be depression, crisis. If the Allies lost the war, the American loans would be lost also. In the last resort, the United States went to war so that America could remain prosperous and rich Americans could grow richer.

America's entry brought limitless resources to the Allied side, but only in a comparatively distant future. The United States had a great navy. They had virtually no army. Millions of men had to be conscripted and trained. There were few munition factories. Tanks, guns, and even rifles had to be supplied by the British and French, not the other way round. No American tanks, and hardly any American aeroplanes, ever reached the Western Front. The Allies now received a new flood of American credit – technically in loans which were to be repaid after the war. But it was hard to spend the money: the Americans needed all their resources for themselves. Thus, America's entry into the war brought at first handicaps, not immediate aid. It was a promissory note for the future, provided that the Allies held on until it could be cashed.

125. The British get American money and American suspicion also.

126, 127.
*Lafayette, we are
here! American
soldiers and
sailors prepare
for action.*

In April 1917 the survival of the Allies seemed uncertain. One great Ally was in process of dropping out of the war. During the winter of 1916–17, food shortage grew worse in the cities of Russia. Early in March there were food riots in Petrograd, the capital. The garrison of elderly soldiers joined in, mainly from alarm that otherwise they might be sent to the front. The Cossacks refused to fire on the rioters. Tsar Nicholas II tried to return to Petrograd from headquarters. Railwaymen stopped his train. He was dragged back to headquarters. The generals there advised him to abdicate. He did so. The Russian Monarchy ended. In Petrograd the real power passed to a Council of Workers' and Soldiers' Deputies, named the Soviet. On its authority, a provisional government of liberal politicians was set up. There was at first no talk of leaving the war. The army was well equipped, though discipline was breaking down. All the muddle was blamed on the fallen Tsar. Surely a free government would do better. Men looked back to the French Revolution, and remembered how the Jacobins had turned France into a great military power. As usual, by trying to learn from history, they learnt the wrong lesson. In the West, the Russian Revolution was hailed with general rejoicing. Not only, it was thought, would the revolution make Russia stronger. The supposed triumph of Russian democracy had removed the one moral flaw on the Allied side. Now there could be no doubt that the Allies were fighting against Imperialism to make the world safe for democracy.

One man thought differently. This was Lenin, the Bolshevik leader, exiled in Zurich. He was not interested in defeating the Germans or in making the world safe for democracy. He wanted to overthrow all existing governments and to establish international Socialism. In his opinion, if revolutionary Russia withdrew from the war, the peoples in every other belligerent country would follow her example. There would be universal revolution, followed by universal peace. The news from Russia threw Lenin into a frenzy of impatience. Far from ending the war, the new rulers of Russia were promising to wage it more vigorously; and they were being supported even by Lenin's Bolshevik followers, under the direction of Stalin. Lenin determined to return to Russia at once. He was not allowed to pass through France and England. Ludendorff, eager only to weaken Russia, agreed to let Lenin pass through Germany. A secret agreement was formally made between Lenin and the German general staff. Lenin and some other Bolsheviks travelled through

128, 129, 130. The Russian Revolution: the people who made it.

131. Lenin (with umbrella) *in Stockholm, the man who mastered it.*

Germany in a sealed train. On 16 April Lenin arrived in Petrograd. He at once denounced the Provisional Government, and began to preach a new revolution. A few weeks later, he received a formidable ally. Trotsky, the greatest orator of the age and soon to prove himself one of the greatest military organizers, arrived from New York, where he had been earning precarious money as a film extra. He was a poor actor. Now the stage of reality was set for an explosion which would overshadow even the war itself.

Few people in the West noticed the first stirring of this second Russian storm. Their eyes were turned towards the Western Front, where Nivelle was about to perform his promised miracle. On 9 April the British opened an offensive at Arras, in order to distract the Germans from noticing the preparations elsewhere. The attack had been carefully rehearsed. For once it was a success. Canadian troops took Vimy Ridge, one of the few hills in the Flanders plain. Then the old story was repeated. The offensive was pushed on too long at the same place. The Germans brought up reserves. Once more the line settled down thicker and stronger than before. The only achievement of the battle of Arras was a fresh butcher's bill: 150,000 British casualties, 100,000 German. All this was

132. Canadians take Vimy Ridge.

preliminary to Nivelle's main plan for an attack on the Aisne. Here the Germans had plenty of warning. A French sergeant-major, captured by the Germans, was found to have full details of Nivelle's plan – perhaps deliberately betrayed by one of his opponents. By 16 April, the allotted day, the Germans had as many divisions on the threatened front as the French. Nivelle's bombardment failed to affect the German machine guns. The French infantry went forward to the old massacre. By the evening the French had advanced 600 yards instead of the six miles which Nivelle had promised. He had failed to perform the miracle after all. Again the old pattern was repeated. Nivelle could not bring himself to admit that his wonderful secret was no secret and that his promised success had failed. The attack was continued for another fortnight with increasing loss. Then it, too, faded away.

Nivelle's brief hour was over. At the end of April he was superseded by Pétain, apostle of the defensive, whose guiding slogan was: 'We must wait for the Americans and the tanks.' Nivelle's failure was no greater than that of others, indeed rather less. He took more ground with fewer casualties than Joffre did in his offensives or than Haig did at Arras. But Nivelle had promised more. Instead he had carried the

exhausted French army beyond breaking point. Widespread mutiny followed. One regiment went to the front bleating like sheep led to the slaughter. Soon fifty-four divisions were refusing to obey orders. Many thousands deserted. Great stretches of front were left undefended, though strangely the Germans never learnt this, and took no advantage of it. Laboriously Pétain restored discipline. Over a hundred thousand soldiers were court martialled. 23,000 were found guilty, though only 432 were sentenced to death and only 55 were officially shot. A good many more were shot without sentence. Another 250 were pounded to death by the artillery according to Henri Barbusse. Leave was doubled, army food was improved. Above all, Pétain conveyed the assurance that there would not be another great offensive. Gradually the French army became again an effective defensive weapon. The offensive spirit of France had gone for many years, perhaps for ever.

An even graver shadow hung over the Allies in the spring of 1917. This was the moment when it looked as though Great Britain would be brought to defeat. The German submarines did all that had been expected of them, and more. In April alone more than a million tons of British and neutral ships were lost. One ship out of every four leaving British ports never

133. The attack that failed: French troops advance during the Nivelle offensive.

134. Not a perfect instrument of war: a tank after the battle of Arras.

135. *British troops go over the top.*

136. *German troops remain in cover.*

came home. Neutral and American ships refused to sail for British ports. There was no hope of replacing the losses with new ships. The British Admiralty were equally at a loss to defeat the German submarines. Jellicoe, now First Sea Lord, told the American Admiral Sims: 'It is impossible for us to go on with the war if losses like this continue.' Sims asked if any solution could be found. Jellicoe replied: 'Absolutely none that we can see now.' Lloyd George had a solution: convoy. The admirals obstinately resisted. They, too, had 'formed a picture' – that convoy would not work. They argued that merchant ships could not keep station, and even called a meeting of merchant captains at the Admiralty which agreed with them. They pleaded that there were too few destroyers to protect the convoys – many of the destroyers being used to protect the Grand Fleet in its harbour at Scapa Flow. They estimated that 2,500 ships left and entered British ports each week – an impossible number to guard. Lloyd George inquired at the Ministry of Shipping and found that the correct figure was less than 140 – the rest was coastal trade. Even now the admirals were not to be moved. They had staked their professional reputation against convoys.

137. Convoy.   At dead of night, Lloyd George consulted junior naval

officers. He accumulated figures and arguments. On 26 April, he went to the Admiralty, armed with his authority as Prime Minister and the backing of the War Cabinet. He took his seat at the head of the Admiralty Board. He gave the formal order that convoys must be instituted. The admirals belatedly discovered that they had been in favour of convoys all along. The first convoys sailed on 10 May. After further orders from Lloyd George, the system became regular for all shipping across the Atlantic. It was an immediate success. On the wide ocean, a hundred ships sailing together were no easier for a submarine to find than one ship sailing alone; and they were a target dangerously protected. With ships sailing on convoy, the rate of loss was one per cent. Without convoy it had been twenty-five per cent. By September, the British and Americans together were building as many ships as the British were losing. By the end of the year, they were sinking German submarines faster than the Germans could build them. The system of convoy was never universal. Ships from lesser ports often tried to come home alone. In the Mediterranean a few Austrian and German submarines reaped a rich harvest. The British had to sustain France and Italy; they had to supply the vast armies in Palestine and at Salonika. Therefore they could not give up

138. *Their enemy, the U-boat.*

using the Mediterranean, as they did in the Second World War. The margin of survival was narrow. At one time there was less than a month's supply of wheat in England. The sinking of a single ship, laden with sugar, meant that jam-making had to be forbidden. But the danger was overcome, thanks solely to Lloyd George. The institution of convoys was his greatest stroke. It ensured that Great Britain would go on to victory, and would survive at any rate the First World War as a Great Power.

By the early summer of 1917 it was becoming clear that the new methods – the German submarines on the one side, Nivelle's plan on the other – had failed to produce quick and decisive victory. The deadlock was back again. There was once more talk of peace. But with a difference. In the preceding autumn the debate whether to seek a peace of compromise was conducted by a few statesmen behind closed doors. The peoples were not consulted; they did not even know that peace was being debated. There was a last splutter of secret diplomacy in March 1917, when Charles, the young Emperor of Austria who had succeeded the aged Francis Joseph in November 1916, tried somehow to save himself and his Empire from ruin. He sounded the British and French governments with vague offers of a

*139. A U-boat
success.*

separate peace. Nothing came of these soundings though they
dragged on for months. The Allies wanted to use Austria-
Hungary against Germany; Charles, despite his imperial title,
could not escape German control. In any case, Italy was the
only Ally actually fighting against Austria-Hungary; and the
Italian statesmen, fearing the disapproval of their own public
opinion, would be content with nothing less than all the gains
promised to them by the treaty of London. The Austrian peace
offer was no more than a deathbed repentance; or something
even later than that – Habsburg independence had already
disappeared. Napoleon had said long ago: 'The Austrians are
always late – with their payments, with their armies, in their
policies.' The Habsburg Monarchy ran true to form until the
end.

The real peace talk of 1917 came from below – from opposition
politicians, Socialist leaders, and shop stewards in the factories.
Though this talk originated in revolutionary Russia, it spread
across the fronts of war. The new democratic rulers of Russia
felt that they could justify remaining in the war only if they
gave it a firm idealistic appeal. They repudiated the secret
treaties, and called for a peace 'without annexations and without indemnities'. This was embarrassing to the other Allied

140. Chancellor Michaelis (fourth from left) receives his instructions and some refreshment.

governments. Ideals were all very well. But they intended to carry off the German colonies and the spoils of the Ottoman Empire; they even had a simple belief that defeated Germany could somehow be made to pay for the war. A peace without annexations and without indemnities would also be a peace without victory. The governments which had promised victory would be discredited. Besides, firm resistance seemed the only way of quelling the existing discontent. Every advocate of peace, or even of moderation, had to be smeared as a defeatist, a pacifist, probably a traitor. In France particularly, the mutinies in the army ruled out any talk of compromise peace by the Government. One murmur of it, and the entire French army would have dissolved. Yet under the surface the talk of peace swelled. Many people were beginning to think that victory was impossible. Others doubted whether it was necessary. Mix the two ideas together, and the result was peace by negotiation.

On top of this was economic discontent, increased by the harsh conditions of the previous winter. There were widespread strikes in Germany, and a mutiny among bored sailors at Kiel. Hoffmann, who had succeeded Ludendorff as Chief-of-Staff on the Eastern Front, made no secret of his belief that Germany could not win the war. He talked to visiting politicians, especially to Erzberger, a prominent member of the Centre party. Erzberger returned to Berlin converted to a compromise peace. He imagined that Bethmann was the chief obstacle to this, and started a campaign for a new Chancellor. To his surprise, this campaign was encouraged by Hindenburg and Ludendorff, though for exactly the opposite reason: they thought Bethmann too soft. Attacked on all sides, Bethmann resigned in July. The politicians hoped to restore former Chancellor, Bülow, who had an undeserved reputation for diplomatic skill. William II disliked Bülow, and rejected the proposal. All were then at a loss. Ludendorff, asked for advice, nominated an unknown bureaucrat, Michaelis, who had been reasonably successful as food controller. In this odd way, Germany ceased to have a civilian head at all for practical purposes. The Reichstag received one consolation. It was allowed to pass a resolution in favour of peace without annexations or indemnities. This Peace Resolution had little effect in other countries. It was too obvious that the only motive of it was a doubt whether the war could be won.

The same doubt existed the other way round in Russia. Popular feeling grew stronger after the revolution. Discipline

141. Chancellor Michaelis accepts the peace resolution of the Reichstag 'as he understands it'.

*142. Kerensky
seeks to inspire
the Russian troops.*

crumbled in the army. Agitation increased in the streets.
Kerensky, a glamorous Socialist, became head of the Government. He imagined that the Russian people could be raised up
by his eloquence. He even imagined that they could be induced
to fight once more against the Germans. In the early days of
July the Russian soldiers lurched against the German lines.
They had a few days of success, and were then overwhelmed
by a German counter-offensive. The German armies reached
the gates of Riga. The Russian soldiers at last lost heart and
interest. They began to go home without waiting for the end
of the war. Kerensky had hoped to restore Russia's fighting
spirit. Instead he destroyed the Russian army. The Germans
were able to move divisions from the Eastern Front, divisions
which they were to use with devastating effect elsewhere.
Kerensky appreciated that his only chance of survival was to
make a separate peace. He appealed to the Allies for permission.
They refused, mainly for fear of the example to their own
peoples. In this way, they helped to push Russia into further
revolution. As a compromise, the Russian Socialists who were
loyal to the Allies proposed an international meeting of Socialists at Stockholm. Russian, British, and French Socialists
should meet Germans and Austrians. The Germans agreed to

come. The French Socialists and the British Labour party were willing. Their governments took fright that the conference might be too successful. The French delegates were refused passports. British delegates received passports, but the seamen refused to carry them. The Stockholm Conference came to nothing. In Russia, this carried popular suspicion of the Allied Powers still further. It stirred the same suspicion among left-wing people in England and France. From this moment there sprang a belief in 'the bosses' war', a war of rival Imperialisms, where the peoples had nothing at stake and were driven to the slaughter for the sake of profits. The men in top hats wanted the war to go on. Men in cloth caps wanted to end it. Lenin wore a cloth cap. Nothing did more to help him to power than the failure of the Stockholm Conference.

It did not need revolutionaries to make the war unpopular. Blunders by the generals could do that by themselves. In the summer of 1917 British strategy, if such it can be called, reached its lowest level. Haig had come through three years of war still in high command and having learnt little from experience. Joffre had gone; Nivelle had gone; even Luden-dorff knew that new methods must be tried. Haig remained convinced that he could break the German lines and win the war by frontal assault. He refused to be discouraged by the failure in the previous year on the Somme. That campaign, he now believed, had been fought in the wrong place, on the in-sistence of Joffre. Besides, the British army had then been raw and inflexible. Haig was not at all sorry that the French army was no longer capable of offensive action and did not demand his cooperation. He could at last pursue the independent strategy of which he had always dreamt. From the moment that he became Commander-in-Chief he looked at the Ypres salient, where British soldiers were constantly being ground to death from two sides. Here, he thought, he could break through and roll up the German line from the north. The position appeared attractive on the map. The British army needed only to advance thirty miles, and it would be at Ostend; another spring, and it would cut all the Belgian railways, on which the Germans depended. The plan was less attractive on closer examination. To the north, the Belgians had broken the dykes and let in the sea; one German flank was therefore secure. At Ypres itself the ground was heavy clay. The water never drained away; bombardment churned it into deep mud. The Germans had been fortifying their line for years past. They no longer

feared French attacks; they had divisions released from the Eastern Front. Haig hoped to win with a bare equality of divisions, and no superiority in tactics.

Later on, Haig manufactured excuses why the Ypres offensive had to be made. He made out that Pétain pleaded for a British offensive in order to divert the Germans from his mutinous army. This was not true. Pétain wanted small actions to keep the Germans busy, not a great offensive which might reduce the British army to the same state of demoralization as his own. Again, Haig recruited Jellicoe to insist that Ostend and Zeebrugge must be taken if the German submarines were to be checked. This, too, was not true. Most German submarines operated from home waters, not from Ostend and Zeebrugge. Haig himself knew that the argument was unsound. He regarded Jellicoe as 'an old woman'; but every argument for the offensive was welcome to him. Haig also made out that this was the last chance for the British to win the war before the Americans arrived. This, too, was an afterthought, and an odd one, when the British claimed that they and the Americans were fighting for the same cause. The truth was simple: Haig had resolved blindly that this was the place where he could win the war. He never inspected the front line. He disregarded the warnings of his own Intelligence Staff against the mud. No one else shared his confidence. Robertson thought that all that would be achieved was killing Germans. Foch said that it was impossible to fight both Boches and *boue* – Germans and mud – and called the projected advance 'a duck's march'. Criticism only made Haig more obstinate.

Lloyd George was a more formidable critic. He was Prime Minister. He could forbid the operation. But Lloyd George was in a weak position, or thought he was. He depended on Conservative support in the House of Commons, and the Conservatives had a blind faith in the military and naval leaders. Greatly daring, Lloyd George had defied Jellicoe and imposed convoys. He could not offend the Conservatives further by going also against Haig. Lloyd George was also discredited by his backing of Nivelle. There events had proved him wrong and Haig right. It was difficult for Lloyd George to go against Haig again. Moreover Lloyd George had come to power on the promise that he would win the war. How could he resist when Haig promised to win the war for him? Haig was skilful in politics, whatever his limitations as a military leader. He coached the war correspondents; conciliated Members of Parliament who visited his headquarters; was in touch with the Liberal Opposition; above all, he enlisted the support of the king. Lloyd George might have resisted if he had had the unanimous backing of the War Cabinet. This instrument broke in his hand. Curzon, who never took a firm line on anything, swallowed Haig's arguments. Smuts, the Boer general whom Lloyd George had brought into the War Cabinet as an independent military adviser, took the side of the British generals whom he had fought, and often beaten, during the Boer War.

Early in June 1917 Haig had a preliminary success before the great argument started, though the success was none of his doing. This was the great mining operation at Messines. Here a ridge, some one hundred and fifty feet high, ran to the south of the Ypres salient. It was in German hands; and from it they could observe everything that was going on behind the British lines. Sir Herbert Plumer, in command, was one of the few sensible British commanders despite his comical military appearance. For two years he had planned to blow the Germans off the ridge. Deep mines were dug, more than one hundred feet beneath the surface; they were stuffed with a million pounds of explosive. Often the Germans, digging somewhat closer to the surface, came so near the British miners that their conversation could be heard without listening apparatus. Often the alarm was raised that the Germans were breaking in and that the mines must be blown. By 6 June 1917 nineteen deep mines had been laid. At 3.10 on the morning of 7 June they were all set off at once. Lloyd George heard the explosion in his room at 10 Downing Street. The German defensive positions were shattered. The British troops walked in and occupied the entire ridge. It was a remarkable success, and a beautiful exercise in siege warfare. But it had disquietening aspects. Two years of preparation and a million pounds of explosive had advanced the British front at most two miles. How long would it take at this rate to get to Berlin?

Haig however could claim that he had improved his position decisively. Now the Germans could not watch his preparations so clearly. He was inclined to hint also that every offensive would be on the Messines pattern, short and sharp. In mid-June 1917 the War Cabinet held prolonged sessions. Haig came from France and was repeatedly cross-examined by Lloyd George. Why should this offensive succeed when all others had failed? Would the French support it? What evidence was there that the Germans were, as Haig claimed, 'demoralized'? Would it not be better to wait for the Americans or to switch

144. Sir Douglas Haig feels the cold.

Allied resources to Italy? This last proposal, Lloyd George's old favourite, was in itself enough to drive Haig on. He preferred an unsuccessful offensive under his own command to a successful one elsewhere under someone else's. At each question Haig grew more confident. There was, he thought, 'a reasonable chance' of reaching Ostend; a little later, 'a very good chance' of complete victory before the end of the year. The War Cabinet were arguing in the dark. The vital facts were concealed from them. They were never told that the Ypres offensive was opposed by the French and that all the British generals except Haig had doubts. They were not told that Haig's own Intelligence Staff had advised against it, and Intelligence in London still more so. They were not told the truth about German strength, nor about the inevitable rain and mud. Moreover the War Cabinet had many other things to do. Economic activity to plan; factory workers to conciliate; convoys to organize; politicians and the newspapers had to be satisfied. Lloyd George had to leave one meeting for his daughter's wedding. The civilian ministers were worn down. Haig was told to prepare for an offensive, and meanwhile the War Cabinet would think again. They never found time to do so. On 25 July Haig announced that all was ready. In answer, the Cabinet sent their 'whole-hearted support'.

Preparations were made on the usual elaborate scale. The Germans, duly warned, prepared also. Their strength grew until it was almost equal to the British. Each side crammed nearly a million men into the Ypres salient. Behind the British lines, divisions of cavalry waited for the breakthrough which never came. On 31 July there began what is officially called the third battle of Ypres, popularly – from its last phase – Passchendaele, most truly by Lloyd George the battle of the mud. Failure was obvious by the end of the first day to everyone except Haig and his immediate circle. The greatest advance was less than half a mile. The main German line was nowhere reached. Rain fell heavily. The ground, churned up by shellfire, turned to mud. Men, struggling to advance, sank up to their waists. Guns disappeared in the mud. Haig sent in tanks. These also vanished in the mud. Imperceptibly Haig changed his tone. The distant objectives, Ostend and Zeebrugge, were forgotten. The only purpose of the battle was to kill Germans and to shake their morale. Yet Ludendorff was so unperturbed that he moved divisions from Russia to the Italian front, not to Flanders.

In mid-August the offensive slackened. Once more Lloyd

George tried to stop it. He crossed to France, and insisted on
going up to the front line. Every fit German was hastily
removed from the prisoner-of-war cages, so that Lloyd George
should believe that the Germans were drawing on their last
reserves of the halt and the lame. Once more he gave way. In
September there were renewed attacks. Haig was convinced
that a German collapse might come 'at any moment'. Lloyd
George, for his part, was convinced that 'he had backed the
wrong horse'. He took advice from two out-of-work generals,
French and Wilson. Both urged that the campaign should be
ended. It still went on. There was another grandiose offensive
in October; a final attack on 7 November, which took the ruins
of Passchendaele, a village which no longer existed. Then Haig
stopped. The campaign 'had served its purpose'. What purpose?
None. The British line stuck out in a sharper and more awkward
salient than before the battle began. All the trivial gains were
abandoned without a fight in order to shorten the line when the
Germans attacked in the following year. The British casualties
were something over 300,000; the German under 200,000 – a
proportion slightly better than on the Somme. Thirty years
later, the British official history turned these figures round:
British losses, 250,000; German 400,000. No one believes these

*145. The 'battle
of the mud'.*

146. *Wipers (Ypres, 1917).*

147. The wicked Hun: a German prisoner taken at Passchendaele.

farcical calculations. After the war also, Ludendorff made out that the prolonged battle had broken the spirit of the German army. This was not serious evidence; it was said only to conceal the fact that he himself had broken his army's spirit by the offensives of 1918. Third Ypres was the blindest slaughter of a blind war. Haig bore the greatest responsibility. Some of the Flanders mud sticks also to Lloyd George, the man who lacked the supreme authority to forbid the battle.

Passchendaele was the last battle in the old style, though no one knew this at the time. Even the generals at last realized that something had gone wrong. On 8 November Haig's Chief-of-Staff visited the fighting zone for the first time. As his car struggled through the mud, he burst into tears, and cried: 'Good God, did we really send men to fight in that?' His companion replied: 'It's worse further up.' Haig alone was undismayed. He went on planning a renewal of the campaign in the spring. The Germans arranged things otherwise. Meanwhile, a demonstration was given, clear for all to see, that there were better ways of fighting the war. Tanks had been useless in the Flanders mud. The tank corps looked for dry hard ground. They found it at Cambrai, forty-five miles south of the battlefield. Haig would allow an attack only when his great offensive had stopped. He had no infantry reinforcements to spare. On 20 November 381 tanks went forward in massed formation without any preliminary bombardment. They crossed all three German lines, and advanced five miles. There was a hole in the German defences four miles wide. This was a greater success than anything achieved on the Somme or in Flanders; and at trifling cost – 1,500 British losses against 10,000 German prisoners and 200 guns. Over in London church bells were rung, for the only time in the war, to celebrate the victory. But no one knew how to use it. The infantry could not keep up with the tanks. The cavalry were easily destroyed by German machine guns. The Germans brought up their reserves. Ten days later they recovered all the lost ground, and a bit more. The great victory turned to disappointment. A court of enquiry solemnly reported that it was all the fault of the men and junior officers; the generals, as usual, were without blame.

Cambrai apart, it was the Germans on whom success seemed to smile in the autumn of 1917. Ludendorff was quite as anxious about the Austrians as Haig was about the French, and perhaps with more reason. He determined to stimulate them with a victory on the Italian front. He moved German divisions from Russia to Italy, not to France. The Italians were already worn

148. Cambrai, the town the tanks did not reach.

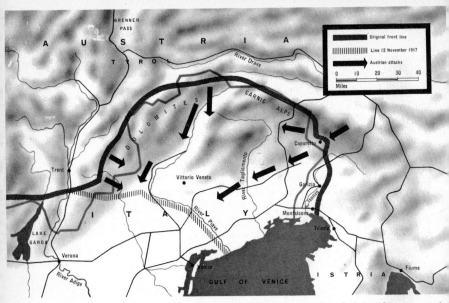

The Italian Front.

down by their fruitless attempts to break into the mountain
barrier which the Austrians held. On 24 October nine Austrian
and six German divisions attacked at Caporetto. The entire
Italian front collapsed. The Italian army went reeling back.
This was again a war of movement, the first in the west since
the battle of the Marne. It took the Germans by surprise. They
had no transport for the infantry, and only horses to move
their guns. They could not keep up with the Italian retreat.
After falling back seventy miles, the Italians stopped on the
Piave, a much shorter line. The line held. To Haig's indignation
five British divisions were sent to Italy; and six French
divisions along with them. The Italian army had lost over
200,000 men in battle: 400,000 had deserted. Yet their army
recovered its spirit to everyone's surprise. Cadorna, the
Commander-in-Chief, was dismissed. Diaz took his place: no
better a general, but at least different. The battle of Caporetto
almost knocked Italy out of the war; instead, strangely enough,
it made the war popular in Italy for the first time.

The Italian disaster had another important effect. On 5
November Allied statesmen met at Rapallo in order to discuss
ways of aiding Italy. Lloyd George repeated his old theme that
the Allies were failing for lack of cooperation; this time his
colleagues agreed with him. They agreed to set up a Supreme

*149, 150. The
battle of Caporetto:
Italians who died
(left); Italians
who surrendered
(below).*

War Council. The three Prime Ministers of Great Britain, Italy, and France would meet regularly at Versailles. Colonel House, the enigmatic Texan, would, they hoped, sit in for President Wilson. At last there would be a unified strategy. In fact the Supreme War Council was largely window-dressing. It served as a meeting-place to discuss general policy; it provided some economic cooperation. The military conduct of the war was at first little affected. The Italians continued to run their own front, though with some assistance from the British and French. There were still two independent armies in France – one under Pétain, the other under Haig. But Lloyd George had struck the first blow at Haig's independence and still more at Robertson's. The Supreme War Council was to have its own military advisers, meeting as a permanent committee. Foch was to be Chairman. Thus Lloyd George would be kept informed of the military situation without having to consult Robertson; and he hoped soon to have an instrument with which to override Haig. Lloyd George once said: 'I was never in favour of frontal attacks, either in politics or in war, if there were a way round.' He had now found the way round Haig's entrenched position.

One Ally was conspicuously missing at Rapallo and from

151. The first men of the new sort: Red Guards in Moscow, November 1917.

the meetings of the Supreme War Council. Russia had fallen out of the war. After the great defeat in July Kerensky tried to restore order in Russia. Many Bolshevik leaders were arrested. Lenin went into hiding in Finland. The Russian army continued to crumble. On 1 September the Germans rounded out their line by taking Riga: the last engagement between the Germans and the old Russian army. Kornilov, who had become Commander-in-Chief, being helpless against the Germans, imagined that he might at least achieve something by crushing the revolution. He planned to march on Petrograd. Kerensky at first encouraged this; then belatedly realized that Kornilov meant to crush not only the Bolsheviks but all semblance of democracy including Kerensky himself. Kerensky raised the alarm. The factory workers were armed on his instructions. Trotsky and the other Bolsheviks were released from prison. The soldiers, sent by Kornilov, made no attempt to enter Petrograd. Many deserted, home to their villages; others joined the revolutionary side. Kornilov was dismissed from his command; arrested; and soon set free again. The Red Guards, under Bolshevik direction, were the only force left in Petrograd. Kerensky and the Provisional Government existed on sufferance.

Yet nothing happened for over six weeks. The Bolsheviks now had a majority on the Petrograd Soviet. They denounced Kerensky, and alleged that he was betraying the revolution, though without specifying to whom. Lenin moved from Finland to a Petrograd suburb. Theoretically he was still in hiding, still clean-shaven as a disguise. He stirred up his Bolshevik followers, insisted that they should seize power. They accepted his direction on paper. In practice they did nothing. Lenin became more and more impatient. Even Trotsky was still content to orate. By a strange twist Kerensky himself sparked off the Bolshevik revolution. At a secret meeting the Central Committee of the Bolsheviks decided to seize power by ten votes to two. The two dissentients, Kamenev and Zinoviev, protested against the decision in the Press. Kerensky imagined that the storm was about to blow, though really effective revolution was no nearer. He decided to take the offensive with a handful of cadets and a battalion of women. On 6 November *Pravda*, the Bolshevik newspaper, was closed on his orders. The Bolsheviks were thus driven into action by Kerensky, not by Lenin. Trotsky ordered Red Guards to rescue *Pravda*. The plan for seizing power was hastily put into operation. The post office, the telegraph exchange, the railway stations, passed into Bolshevik hands. Kerensky left Petrograd, his car flying an American flag, in order to rally the loyal troops in the provinces. He found no loyal troops, and disappeared from history. In the late evening of 7 November Red Guards captured the Winter Palace, and arrested the members of the Provisional Government. Such was the Bolshevik revolution. It cost the lives of six Red Guards, two killed accidentally by their own comrades. No one was killed on the side of the Provisional Government.

That same evening the second Soviet Congress of workers, peasants, and soldiers from all Russia met at Smolny, a former girls' school in the suburbs of Petrograd. The delegates were informed, to their surprise, that all power was in their hands. They were also informed that a Soviet government was already in existence, and they accepted, without query, the list of commissars which the Bolsheviks had drawn up. Lenin became Chairman; Trotsky Commissar for Foreign Affairs. Trotsky thought this a temporary job. He said: 'I shall issue a few proclamations and then shut up shop.' The officials refused to work with the new government. Red Guards blew open the vaults of the Imperial Bank, and forced the archives of the Foreign Ministry. Lenin set out to win the masses. At his first

152. The all-Russia Congress of Soviets declares that the war is over.

appearance before the Soviet Congress, he announced, when the applause had died down: 'We shall now proceed to the building up of Socialism.' Like Trotsky, he thought this the affair of a few days – some proclamations, the factories handed over to the workers, the rich deprived of their money, and then Socialism would have arrived. The factory workers were already largely on the Bolshevik side. It was more urgent to win over the peasants. Lenin hastily drafted a Decree on Land, authorizing the peasants to seize the land of landowners and to divide it among themselves. Though this was contrary to Bolshevik policy, it ensured that the peasants took the Bolshevik side during the ensuing civil war.

Lenin's most pressing object in seizing power was to end the war. This too, he thought, was a matter of a few proclamations. On 8 November he read at the Soviet Congress his Decree on Peace. There should be an immediate armistice on all fronts; then negotiations for a peace without annexations or indemnities. The Great Powers were invited to surrender not only the conquests which they had made during the war, but also the colonies which they had held before it; the peace should be 'fair for all nationalities without exception'. Lenin expected resistance from what he called the Imperialist governments;

153. They asked for bread and got revolutionary propaganda: distribution of Pravda *in Moscow, winter 1917.*

154. *Trotsky, triumphant leader of the Red Army, ignores the danger from Stalin (extreme right).*

'but we hope that revolution will soon break out in all the belligerent countries'. He appealed particularly to the workers of England, France, and Germany – heirs of the Chartists, of the great French Revolution, and of the struggle against Bismarck. A few days later Trotsky began to publish the secret treaties, sending them out to the world from the Petrograd wireless station.

The German Government were ready to respond. They wanted to be finished with the Eastern Front; and agreed to an armistice, though they did not take seriously the talk about no annexations and no indemnities. The Western governments were in a more embarrassing position. They claimed to be fighting for the same idealistic principles which Lenin had announced so tactlessly. They did not believe that Germany would accept these principles without defeat; nor did they themselves intend to apply them strictly. Yet they had to contend with a great desire for peace in their own countries. British and French Socialists applauded the Bolshevik programme, though shocked at the undemocratic way in which Lenin and Trotsky had come to power. Nor was agitation for peace confined to the working classes. On 29 November Lord Lansdowne, a former Foreign Secretary, published a letter in the *Daily Telegraph*. The war, he argued, could not be won without ruining civilization; therefore negotiations should be opened for a compromise peace. He did not explain how the German Government were to be brought to the same enlightened view. Within the War Cabinet Lord Milner suggested, more realistically, that the Germans should be bought out of their western conquests by being given a free hand to do what they liked with Russia.

There was trouble also in France, where the Socialists became increasingly restive as the year wore on. In September their ministers left the Government. The last fragments of 'sacred union' were thus dissolved. The Socialists even proposed that plebiscites should be held in Alsace and Lorraine before the two provinces returned to France. Nationalist opinion was outraged. On 13 November Prime Minister Painlevé was defeated in the Chamber. President Poincaré pondered the decisive question – should he appoint Caillaux, the advocate of a compromise peace, or Clemenceau, a man whom he hated but a resolute warrior? Being himself from Lorraine and a fierce Nationalist, Poincaré appointed Clemenceau. His was not another parliamentary government. It was a war dictatorship. When Clemenceau first appeared before the Chamber on

155. Clemenceau takes a walk at the front.

20 November, he said; 'You ask what are my war aims? Gentlemen, they are very simple: *Victory*.' And on 8 March 1918: 'Home policy? I wage war. Foreign policy? I wage war. All the time I wage war.' Clemenceau disregarded the politicians. He appointed loyal satellites as ministers. He arrested Caillaux and other supporters of a compromise peace, and accused them of treason or of correspondence with the enemy. Though most of the charges did not stick, they stirred patriotic emotions into enthusiasm for Clemenceau.

This was not the moment to put before the British and French governments the idea of an armistice or of an idealistic peace. The Supreme War Council met on 29 November. The Bolshevik suggestion of an armistice, or even of negotiations, was rejected out of hand, amid much rumbling against Russian treachery. No doubt Clemenceau and Lloyd George genuinely believed that no fair or even tolerable peace was possible until Germany had been defeated. But they were also aware that they owed their own position to repeated promises of total victory. They supposed that they would defeat the Socialists and so 'save society' by going on with the war; whereas anything less than victory would justify Socialist criticisms. These arguments did not move consciously in their heads. Both men were skilled political tacticians; both rated their own abilities highly; both loved power. A strong line raised cheers. Attempts at moderation would provoke a storm in Parliament and in the Press. It is easy for statesmen to be courageous at the expense of others; difficult for them to be sensible – and perhaps there was at this time no sensible course. At any rate, the decision was taken quickly and firmly: a sharp and final negative to the Bolshevik proposal. Moreover it followed logically that anyone advocating a peace without victory was himself a Bolshevik – or next door to it: a harsh verdict on poor Lord Lansdowne. His argument about preserving civilization was stood on its head. In order to save society from Bolshevism the war must be carried on to the bitter end. Lloyd George, Clemenceau, and for that matter Ludendorff, all believed that victory would be the best security for the established order, though they could not of course all three be satisfied in this aim.

Once the Allies had rejected the proposals for a general armistice, the Bolsheviks went ahead with negotiating a separate peace. An armistice between Russia and Germany was signed on 15 December. Peace negotiations followed at Brest Litovsk. The Bolsheviks made a last gesture to their former allies by stipulating that no German troops should be moved from the Eastern Front after the armistice came into force. Hoffmann agreed to this condition and evaded it by moving his troops beforehand. The Western Allies waxed more indignant than ever over this open betrayal. None of the British or French statesmen grasped that Russia's withdrawal from the war was not the work of the Bolsheviks. The entire Russian nation had stopped fighting; the Russian army did not exist; all that remained was to set some limit of agreement to the advance of the German army. This was what the Bolsheviks were trying to do. The British and French imagined that somewhere was to be found a great body of Russians eager to resume the war. They solemnly divided Russia into zones of influence where each would stir up warlike feeling and resistance to the Bolsheviks, which they regarded as the same thing: the Ukraine to France, the Caucasus to Great Britain. In this way the Allies stumbled into a new war without knowing it – a war supposedly directed against the Germans, but really against the new political system in Russia. The Iron Curtain of later days was already in process of formation.

This suited Clemenceau. He wanted the subversive ideas of the Bolsheviks kept far from France. Also he was glad to see the Russians punished both for failing as allies and, even more shocking, for repudiating their debts to French investors. Lloyd George was less content. He needed to conciliate Labour opinion in Great Britain, particularly when the unions had to be cajoled into releasing more men from the factories to replace those whom Haig had lost in Flanders. Lloyd George therefore produced a moderate and idealistic statement of British war aims – not quite 'no annexations and no indemnities', but next door to it: no dismemberment of the Habsburg Monarchy, no partition of the Ottoman Empire among the victors. Over in Washington President Wilson was even more distressed at the breach between Russia and her former allies. Wilson felt uncomfortably that Lenin's Decree on Peace was almost what he ought to have been saying himself. He even fancied that the Russians might be induced to resume the war if its objects were presented in enlightened enough terms. On 8 January 1918, Wilson announced the Fourteen Points – sketch of a programme for peace which would, he hoped, make another war impossible. Like Lenin he repudiated the secret treaties, and demanded self-determination. Wilson's new contribution was a League of Nations, providing security for great and small.

Wilson's programme was almost as unwelcome to the Allies as Lenin's had been. For obvious reasons they could not say so. Clemenceau contented himself with remarking of the Fourteen Points: 'The Lord God had only ten.' In more public pronouncements, the Allies stressed the righteousness of their cause. Faced with the disappointments of the year, they even consoled themselves with the doctrine that Right would triumph over Might.

Their disappointment was manifest. There had been no decisive victory on the Western Front: instead two disastrous failures which had shaken the spirits of both French and British armies. Italy seemed to be running a race towards catastrophe with Austria-Hungary which she might well win. Russia was out of the war, but unfortunately not out of existence. Bolshevik propaganda poisoned the air impartially for Allies and Germans alike. The British had one success to score. On 9 December Allenby, who had been sent to retrieve an earlier failure in Palestine, received the surrender of Jerusalem. Two days later he entered the Holy City on foot, its first Christian master since the Crusades. A few weeks previously the British announced that there was to be a National Home for the Jews in Palestine – thus winning, they hoped, the support of Jews both in America and central Europe, and also ensuring that Palestine would not be allotted to the French. Lloyd George, with his biblical upbringing, was delighted with the capture of Jerusalem. It caused little distress to the Germans.

For them the year had gone well, or at any rate better than they had expected. They had inflicted a great defeat on the Italians; their position in France was stronger than at the beginning of the year. Above all, they were free at last from the burden of 'war on two fronts'. The submarine campaign had not come up to expectations; American forces were accumulating and were beginning to reach France in large numbers. But Ludendorff, inspired with the successes of the year, hoped to improve on them in 1918. He believed that he could get Russia finally and formally out of the war before the United States were effectively in; then he would win a decisive victory on the Western Front before the Americans arrived. The Allies, on the other hand, hoped to keep a bit of something going in Russia, and, more pertinently, to keep going themselves until the Americans arrived. Both Germans and Allies believed that they would win before general collapse pulled all their countries into Bolshevik ruin, or even before they were compelled to accept Wilson's programme of an idealistic peace. Ludendorff,

156. *The end of infidel rule: Turkish troops leave Jerusalem, December 1917.*

157, 158. Germans in Russia : dictating terms, counting bodies.

Lloyd George, and Clemenceau, though fighting each other, were still more concerned that victory should not go to either Lenin or Wilson. The European Powers, though enemies, were basically in agreement; the two World Powers, Russia and America, were also near to agreement if they did but know it. However Lenin and Wilson, the two Utopians, did not manage to join hands.

159. The spectre of Bolshevism, is haunting Europe: Lenin speaks, 1918.

1918

The war had now, as it were, spun round on its axis. Russia was out; the United States were in. There were new tactics, new weapons. New principles swept across the world. Little of this was obvious to the peoples involved. The trenches offered the same dreary mixture of danger and discomfort. At home there was the same hard round of work in the munitions factories and short supplies in the shops. In most belligerent countries, however, food supplies were rather better than in the year before. Distribution, not supply, now tended to break down. The French were never short of food, only of products from abroad such as coffee. The Germans and Austrians took wheat from the Russian territory which they occupied; and they took still more after the signature of peace with the Bolsheviks. In both countries the bread ration was increased more than once during the course of 1918. The worst danger for Great Britain had been in the early days of the submarine campaign, during the spring months of 1917. This campaign was now held in check; and the shortage of some foods had been overcome also. Rationing of meat, sugar, and butter, though not of bread, was introduced only in February 1918, when the real danger was over; and its introduction actually increased such shortage as there was. Perhaps the bureaucrats in the Ministry of Food had to justify their existence and their elaborate plans; or perhaps rationing was produced as an instalment of social equality, to offset profiteering. Whatever the explanation, British rationing lacked a practical economic motive. However, thanks to rationing, food queues disappeared. War settled down into a routine at home as much as it had long been in the trenches. Even in September 1918 Northcliffe, the great newspaper proprietor, and presumably a well-informed man, said to one of his subordinates: 'None of us will live to see the end of the war.'

Half the war ended in March 1918, at any rate on paper. Immediately after signing an armistice, the former combatants on the Eastern Front plunged into the intricacies of peace making. The peace conference met at Brest Litovsk, drab and desolate fortress town in eastern Poland. The Russian delegation was composed of Bolshevik intellectuals and a supposedly typical peasant whom they had collected at random on the way to the railway station. Cheerfully mixing white wine and red, he could drink any German officer under the table. These gay scenes soon changed. Trotsky arrived to take charge. He enforced the class war whatever had happened to the other one. Kühlmann, the German Secretary of State, attempted to speak to Trotsky when standing next to him in the gentlemen's lavatory. Trotsky gave a start of horror as though he had been accosted. Though the Russian army was in dissolution, Trotsky thought he could win by the use of the 'dialectic'. Day after day, he wrangled with Kühlmann over the principle of self-determination which the Germans, too, had theoretically accepted. What was 'the will of the people'? How could it be ascertained? How applied? Could it be freely expressed when German armies were still in occupation? Kühlmann delighted in these arguments. Czernin, Foreign Minister of Austria-Hungary, writhed. He wanted to get the food trains running to Vienna, though he also wanted to acquire territory for his august master. Hoffmann, the German general in command, writhed also.

Trotsky believed that he had a more powerful weapon than argument. He hoped that the German and Austrian workers would respond to the Peace Decree and would rebel as the Russian workers had done. He was not disappointed. Germany and Austria-Hungary were swept by strikes. The workers were given more wages, even more food. At the end of January the strikes died away. Trotsky returned to Petrograd and consulted his Bolshevik colleagues. Most of them wished to defy the Germans and to fight a romantic revolutionary war. Lenin, alone once more, insisted that the soldiers had voted against war. He was asked, How? He answered: 'They have voted with their feet by running away.' Trotsky proposed a compromise: they should reject the German terms and merely announce that the war was over. He promised to support Lenin if this bluff failed to work. Lenin reluctantly agreed. Trotsky reappeared at Brest Litovsk. On 10 February he played his great stroke. 'No war – no peace.' The Bolshevik delegates broke up the conference and departed. Kühlmann wanted to accept the situation. After all the Germans had got what they wanted: the war in the east was over. Hoffmann refused. Legalistic, like most generals, he could not imagine an end to a war without a treaty. Besides, he was maddened by Trotsky's defiance and wished to humiliate him. The Germans denounced the armistice. Their armies moved relentlessly forward. There was nothing to stop them except space. It seemed that Petrograd itself would fall.

Hastily the Bolsheviks moved the capital to Moscow. There they debated once more the question of peace or war. Trotsky still hankered after resistance. He sought out the Allied representatives, inquired what possibilities there were of aid. The Allied governments had not recognized the Bolsheviks. They wanted to get rid of this wicked system with its advocacy of Socialism and an idealistic peace. Even their encouragement of resistance was mainly a device for ruining the Bolsheviks in another way. In any case the British and French had no troops to send, and little means of sending even supplies. All they could offer was Japanese assistance in the Far East. This offer alarmed the Bolsheviks more than no offer at all. They knew that the Japanese were only interested to grab Russian territory for themselves. Besides, the idea was unworkable: it was impossible for the Japanese to get anywhere near Europe even if they had been willing. After fierce debate Lenin got his way. Bolshevik delegates returned to Brest Litovsk. They refused to discuss, or even to read the terms. On 3 March they signed, in silence, the dictated peace of Brest Litovsk. Russia lost all the conquests which the tsars had made during the last two hundred years. The Baltic states, Poland, even the Ukraine, became theoretically independent. In practice, they were added to the German Empire; and German princes quarrelled over supposedly vacant thrones. Yet Russia lost little territory inhabited by Russians; and the Allies, though holding up their hands in horror, maintained the frontiers of Brest Litovsk, except for the Ukraine, after Germany was defeated. The Russians had to wait for Stalin and the Second World War to put themselves back where the tsars had been.

The Allies made much of Bolshevik betrayal and of the lost Eastern Front. In reality, Russia was incapable of further fighting; and the Allies were incapable of helping her. Sympathy was their only weapon, not impotent abuse. Instead they tried to stir up counter-revolution, and thus consolidated Bolshevik hostility against them. The Germans did not do much better. They, too, distrusted the Bolsheviks and even feared them. German divisions remained on the Eastern Front – some to extract grain from the peasants, the rest as a precaution against the imaginary Red army. Bolshevik propaganda spread into central Europe as the prisoners of war returned. In the West the treaty of Brest Litovsk was held up as an example of what the Germans would do if they were victorious. The Germans were to learn the truth of Radek's bitter cry: 'One day the Allies will impose a Brest Litovsk on you.' Undeterred, the Germans made a similar punitive peace with Rumania; and counted mistakenly on a flow of Rumanian oil.

At any rate, the Germans had the situation which they had long craved: they were free to fight a war on one front. As early as 11 November 1917, a fateful date, Ludendorff had resolved to win decisive victory in the west during the coming year. There were plausible arguments for doing this. Time was working against the Germans. The Allied blockade was causing grave shortages, more of industrial raw materials than of food. American troops were arriving in France in growing number. Germany's associates, and particularly Austria-Hungary, were creaking at the joints. This would be the last chance for knocking France and Great Britain out of the war. Yet these arguments were little more than pretexts, like those which Haig had used to justify the Flanders offensive in the previous year. The German army was quite strong enough to maintain a successful defensive; and if by 1919 the Americans came to dominate the scene, their power would be used not to destroy Germany but to impose an enlightened peace on Germans and Allies alike. This is what Ludendorff really feared. Most Germans might welcome a truly conciliatory peace; he and the great general staff would be ruined politically if they returned with less than victory. On a more practical basis, Hindenburg and Ludendorff were inspired to aim at complete victory by their previous success in beating off the British attacks in Flanders – quite the reverse of Haig's claim that they had been discouraged. Most of all, Ludendorff was a general just like Haig; and could not resist the prospect of total victory once he had constructed it in his own mind.

The Germans had no new weapons with which to mount an offensive. Their general staff placed no urgent orders for tanks until August 1918. There was no mechanized transport for the infantry. Nor had Ludendorff much superiority in men. The opposing forces on the Western Front were about equal, even after the Germans brought over fifty-two divisions from the Eastern Front. Ludendorff's asset was in new tactics which recovered the lost art of surprise. The attacking forces took up their positions secretly by night. The trains behind the German lines kept up an incessant shunting to obscure the movements that were taking place. There was to be no preliminary bombardment. Light forces were to go forward, finding weak spots, instead of the massed infantry breaking themselves against strong ones. Ludendorff's strategy also had a novel aspect. He saw the key to the front just south of Ypres, exactly as Haig had done the other way round. A German breakthrough here would not only reach the Channel ports. It would also turn the entire flank and roll up the front from the north. But Ludendorff planned this as his second move. His first was to be further south, where the British and French armies joined. This would distract British attention from the vital point. Geographically, not of course in method, Ludendorff planned first a Somme and then a Passchendaele in quick succession; an ambitious programme which he almost achieved.

The Allied generals appreciated that some German offensive was being prepared. Even Haig recognized by the end of 1917 that he could not renew the attacks in Flanders which he had reluctantly broken off. Pétain set up a cry that the British should take over a further stretch of the French front. Haig, recently so confident, now insisted that he needed every man. Here seemed an opening for the Supreme War Council at Versailles. It proposed to set up an inter-allied reserve of some thirty divisions under its own control. In this way Foch, Chairman of the Military Committee, would really determine strategy. Unified command would arrive by the back door. Sir

161. *Ludendorff considers how to win the war.*

William Robertson displayed his usual powers of dogged resistance. He wrote secretly to Asquith, stirred a campaign in the Press, summoned Haig from France. Lloyd George's fate was once more in the balance. Sharp words were exchanged in the House of Commons. When the king backed the generals, Lloyd George answered by threatening to resign. George V gave way. Haig, the king's man, adroitly gave way too. Robertson left office all alone: this advocate of the Western Front received the command in eastern England – a good joke at his expense, possibly deliberate. Lloyd George had survived a crisis, though he was no nearer getting rid of Haig. During the excitement the general reserve was forgotten. Haig and Pétain insisted that they had no troops to spare; they agreed simply on mutual support should it become necessary. The warnings of German preparation multiplied. Some British Intelligence officers got near its exact time and place. Haig disregarded these warnings. He kept the bulk of his forces concentrated in the north. He recognized correctly that this was the vital spot, and so failed to allow for Ludendorff's preliminary blow. In any case, Haig was still dreaming that he might take the offensive himself after all; and this of course had to be around Ypres. Later, after the German success, Haig

162. The Imperial War Cabinet and dog.

shifted the blame from himself to Lloyd George. He claimed that the army in France had been deliberately starved of men in order to prevent a new offensive. The legend lingers to the present day. The decision to keep men in England was taken by the War Office. No doubt Lloyd George might have over-ruled the War Office; and no doubt, lacking faith in Haig, he did not try to do so. Nevertheless the German victories were not due to a shortage of men on the British side. The men were there, but in the wrong place. As a further stroke of weakness, they were disposed in the wrong way. The British had imitated the German defence in depth, and changed it for the worse. Instead of treating the first or forward zone as a mere buffer, held by few men, they put a third of their force in it, and thus lost a third of their strength before the real battle started.

The Germans had a final advantage for which no one can be blamed and which no one foresaw. On 21 March 1918 there was dense fog. By chance this was the predestined day for the German attack on the Somme. The German infantry overran the British machine-gun posts almost unobserved. Soon the whole line began to crumble. The British troops were wartime soldiers, most of their officers included. They had been trained to hold a trench and occasionally to attack from it. They had no experience of open warfare, and were bewildered when driven from their carefully prepared system of trenches. They retreated a great distance, learning as they went. Haig's reserves were far away in the north. Pétain fulfilled his promise and sent reserves – ultimately indeed more than he had promised, thirteen divisions instead of six. But he also made it clear that his main concern was to cover Paris, whereas Haig was preparing to fall back on the Channel ports. The British and French armies were in danger of being split asunder. Haig belatedly appreciated the virtues of the Supreme Command which he had previously opposed. He telegraphed urgently to the War Cabinet. Lord Milner came over.

On 26 March, while the British Fifth Army was still reeling back, British and French leaders met at Doullens. As Pétain came into the room, he pointed to Haig and whispered to Clemenceau: 'There is a general who will have to surrender in the open field, and I after him.' A few minutes later, Foch bounced in full of confidence. He said: 'Why aren't you fighting? I would fight without a break. I would fight in front of Amiens . . . I would fight all the time.' Milner took Clemenceau out of the room and said: 'The British generals accept the

command of General Foch.' Haig eagerly agreed. The decision was made without consulting the War Cabinet. Foch was entrusted with 'the coordination of the Allied armies'. His powers soon grew. On 3 April he was given 'the strategic direction of military operations'. This time the Americans accepted Foch's authority also. On 14 April he received the title of 'Commander-in-Chief of the Allied armies in France'. Theoretically he stood above all the Allied authorities. In practice Clemenceau tried to order him about, and sometimes succeeded. Moreover Foch could only persuade; he could not compel. He was, in his own words, 'conductor of an opera who beats time well'. Actually he was a bit more: a conductor who had his own instrument. Though he could not command the fighting armies, he controlled their reserves and could decide when these should be used. Previously each Allied commander had flung in his reserves at once when menaced by a German attack. Now Foch held the reserves back, despite agonized cries for help from first Haig and then Pétain. When he used them it was for a counter-attack, not simply to stop up a hole. Foch's control of the reserves goes far to explain the apparent paradox in the campaign of 1918. The Germans made far greater advances than ever before and far greater gains in

163. The offensive which lost Germany the war.

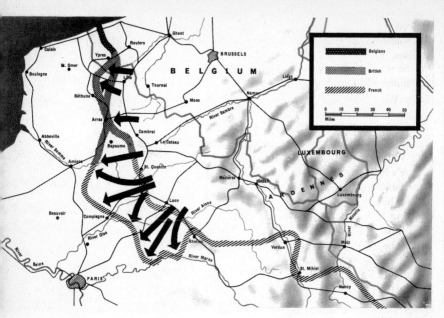

The German offensive, 1918.

terms of territory; they were beaten decisively nevertheless. By allowing the Germans to advance, Foch actually restored the war of movement, which was the only way in which the war could be won. Apart from controlling the reserves, Foch had to stand aside and hope for the best. There was no Supreme Headquarters in any serious sense, and no combined staff. The Allied commanders rarely consulted each other. Haig, Pétain, and Pershing the American commander, only met Foch once to discuss strategy. Even then, there was never a fully coordinated plan of campaign. Three separate armies fought to the end.

Meanwhile the impetus of the German advance gradually ran down. Allied reserves arrived faster by train than the attacking infantry could move forward on foot. Ludendorff, excited by success, broke his own rule: he went on attacking even when he met obstinate resistance. On 28 March he expanded his offensive northwards towards Arras, and imagined that his armies would reach Amiens at a bound. At Arras there were strong British forces. No German advance was made. The Germans were pushing into a sack, the sides of which were thickening around them. They had acquired a dangerous bulge or salient instead of a breakthrough. On 5 April the offensive was halted. The Germans had inflicted great losses. They had suffered great losses also, perhaps greater. Moreover the German soldiers were discouraged when they saw the lavish British supplies. They could not help feeling that they had already lost the war. In England Lloyd George responded vigorously to the challenge as he always did. On 23 March he went himself to the War Office, where he found confusion and dismay. On his own authority he dispatched all available troops to France, and increased the cross-Channel transports threefold. Then he descended on the Foreign Office, and sent a telegram to President Wilson, appealing for immediate American aid. Lloyd George's intervention in this crisis was as dramatic and almost as decisive as had been his order for convoys in the previous year. The Americans responded to his appeal. Previously Pershing had insisted that his troops would fight only as an independent army. Now he agreed temporarily that they should be brought as reinforcements into the British and French armies.

Ludendorff was still eager for his second blow in the north. But his forces were running down. He could only supply eleven fresh divisions instead of the thirty-five originally planned. The name of the operation was changed significantly from St George to Georgette. On 9 April the Germans attacked in

164. They barred the way to Paris: French troops after the German offensive, May 1918.

165, 166. Horrors of war, 1918: French refugees; French cow.

Flanders towards Hazebrouck. They had an unexpected stroke of luck. The line here was held only by one Portuguese division, tired, depressed, and due for withdrawal. We need not linger over the questions why and when Portugal entered the war. At any rate the miserable troops were there. They broke on the first onslaught. The Germans made a hole thirty miles wide, though only five miles deep. Ludendorff was again excited by success and began to feed in all his available reserves. The British abandoned Passchendaele which they had won at such bitter cost in the previous year. Haig feared for the Channel ports. On 12 April he issued his famous order of the day: 'With our backs to the wall and believing in the justice of our cause each one of us must fight to the end.' This had much effect in England, though it provoked little except derision among the fighting troops. Foch remained undismayed. He insisted that this attack was 'not the real thing'. As usual, he wanted to keep the reserves for an offensive of his own. In the end Foch put in four French divisions. By 29 April the German attack had been stayed. Once more Ludendorff had been tempted to go on too long, and this time had little to show for it. His resolve was still unshaken: somehow he would break through the Flanders line. He decided that a further, and more elaborate feint was necessary. He therefore projected a great diversionary offensive against the French, which would pull their reserves away from the north. After this 'Hagen', the decisive operation, could at last be delivered, and the British front rolled up.

The preparations for this new German plan took nearly a month. The German soldiers had started the campaign of 1918 in high spirits. They were now being worn down by their own offensives, just as the French and the British had been worn down before them. The constant shifts of front no doubt made sense to Ludendorff. They bewildered the ordinary fighting-man, who only grasped that the decisive victory, so often promised, had not arrived after all. The Allied armies, on the other hand, gained new confidence from each blow that was beaten off, again just as the Germans had done in previous years. Joffre, Haig, and Nivelle had nearly lost the war by their repeated offensives. Now Ludendorff was imitating them. Danger spurred the Allies in other ways. They seized upon weapons hitherto regarded as shockingly immoral. Lord Northcliffe, the Press Lord, was called in to conduct political warfare. The German soldiers were bombarded with democratic propaganda and cruder appeals to desert. The appeals met with little response until seconded by defeat in the field. Northcliffe and

168. British troops improvise a trench.

others found a more exposed target in Austria-Hungary. The Habsburg fumblings towards a negotiated peace dragged on until the news of Ludendorff's first successes. Then the Emperor Charles and his advisers dreamt that they might survive the war after all, if only as German satellites; they even dreamt of a unified central Europe under German orders.

The Allies answered by a full-throated appeal to the nationals of Austria-Hungary other than the Germans and Hungarians. The war became at last a subversive operation, with the most respectable statesmen, such as Balfour, preaching revolution. The Czechs asked to be recognized as an Allied nation. They produced a new, and irresistible, attraction. Czech prisoners of war in Russia had been assembled in order to return home across Siberia and the Pacific. In the general confusion, they organized their own legion, organized their own movement along the Trans-Siberian railway. At first the Bolsheviks regarded them with a friendly eye, then came to believe that they were secret agents for counter-revolution or Allied intervention. On 14 May Czechs and Hungarians quarrelled at the dreary Siberian station of Chelyabinsk. The Czech legion won control. The Bolshevik Government, in alarm, ordered that the legion should be disarmed. Instead the Czech legion seized

169. Old methods are best: the pigeon post in operation, April 1918.

the entire railway from Samara to Irkutsk. With this the Czechs became heroes in the Allied eyes: representatives of a great democratic principle, yet also the spearhead of intervention against the Bolsheviks. Allied intervention in Russia could be presented as a move to rescue the Czechs, instead of as an anti-Socialist crusade. Even President Wilson swallowed this argument, and agreed reluctantly to a Japanese intervention in Siberia. In this way the Allies got a second war on their hands before they had finished the first. The Czechs received their rewards. They were recognized as a people struggling to be free; soon, under the guise of Czechoslovaks, as a people who had established the right to their own state. This spelled doom to the Empire of the Habsburgs. It could survive loss of territory on the fringe to Serbs or Rumanians; an independent Czechoslovakia cut out its heart. In this strange way, the deathblow to an empire centuries old was struck far away on the railway platform at Chelyabinsk.

The only chance for the Habsburg Monarchy lay now with a German victory, not in a separate peace. Imperial authority broke down in Austria-Hungary not so much from actual hardship as from general loss of faith. Though food supplies were adequate with the wheat from the Ukraine, men no longer observed the rules. The wheat-trains were pillaged. Armed bands of deserters and of prisoners of war, returned from Russia, roamed the countryside, plundering as they went. It was no longer only exiles who prophesied the fall of the Empire. Leading politicians spoke of it openly in the Austrian Parliament. The newspapers treated it as something inevitable, like a fall of snow in the coming winter. Even the Emperor Charles was psychologically packing his bags for exile.

While the war in France mounted to its critical peak, the other services developed a new activity. During 1917 the German High Seas Fleet had hardly moved. In April 1918 Admiral Scheer resolved to catch one of the British convoys from Norway – convoys vital for their supply of pit-props, so vital indeed that they were accompanied by units from the Grand Fleet. He sailed on 23 April, a day too late for one convoy, a day too early for another. At exactly the same time, the British were more successful, though not completely so. Rear-Admiral Keyes attacked Zeebrugge and Ostend to make them unusable by German submarines. Three block-ships were sunk at Zeebrugge, though they did not quite close the channel. This was one of the most daring operations of the war, though quite pointless:

170, 171. Paris under bombardment and the bombarding gun.

172. The daring stroke that failed : British ships do not quite block the harbour at Zeebrugge.

German submarines hardly used the two harbours. More effective, though less dramatic, was the line of deep mines laid by Keyes across the Straits of Dover. The British and Americans also laid a line of mines all the way from the Orkneys to the Norwegian coast – a line never fully completed. Shipping losses went on at a heavy rate, but new ships were built at a greater.

The German air raids on England ceased in May 1918, though not before they had provoked a hysterical demand to intern all enemy aliens in retaliation. This demand was voiced by Pemberton Billing, 'member for air', and hero of a famous libel case in which he alleged that the names of 47,000 prominent Englishmen were recorded in a Black Book of homosexual practices, held by the Germans. The French had hitherto escaped air attacks. On Good Friday the first shells fell in Paris from an enormous German gun, Big Bertha, seventy-one miles away. Thereafter Paris was regularly bombarded with much loss of life, though no crippling damage. One other date deserves to be recorded. On 1 April 1918 the Royal Air Force came into existence – the first independent air force in the world. Most of its immediate duty was to assist the British army in France. But it also launched an independent bombing offensive; and was on the point of attacking even Berlin when the armistice came. This unfulfilled attack left a legacy for the future in the untested belief that bombing could win a war unaided.

All these were side shows to the great battle in France. Throughout May German forces moved south in fantastic secrecy which baffled Allied Intelligence. Ludendorff planned to attack on the Aisne, scene of Nivelle's failure in 1917. Once more, luck favoured him. The Allies had not expected an attack, at this point – so much so that the line was held by five exhausted British divisions who had been sent to rest there after the fighting in Flanders. Moreover the old-fashioned French general in command neglected previous experience and put all his men in the front line. On 27 May fourteen German divisions broke right through and advanced ten miles in a single day, the biggest such advance since the remote time of August 1914. By 3 June the Germans reached the Marne and were only fifty-six miles from Paris. Once more Ludendorff was lured on by success. He pushed in new forces which ground to a halt as Foch at last moved his reserves. Once more the Germans had marched into a sack; they had not broken the French front.

They had not even drawn in the bulk of Foch's reserves which were still kept in the north. All the same, the German advance caused plenty of alarm. Terrifying memories of 1914 were stirred when 'the Marne' appeared again in French newspapers. The Chamber of Deputies grew critical. Clemenceau stood firm, and defended Foch even at risk to his own prestige. Many subordinate generals were dismissed, quite in the old style. To make matters worse, the armies were struck by an epidemic, known as Spanish influenza, the greatest killer of the century. It swept across the world, ravaged the civilians during the autumn. In India alone more people died from it than were killed on all the battlefields throughout the four years of war. Men grew feverish as the war reached its climax.

Decision rested with Ludendorff for the last time. Victory had eluded him despite repeated success. He talked of playing political warfare like his enemies, and sapping their nerve by misleading offers of a compromise peace. But when Kühlmann, the German Secretary of State, tried this move publicly on 24 June, Ludendorff feared that it was German nerves which would be sapped. Kühlmann was hastily forced from office. The last slight chance of negotiation was lost. German policy formally renewed the intention of holding on to German conquests,

173. A London bus is protected against Spanish influenza.

especially in Belgium. Thus the invasion of Belgium, which originally lured the Germans with a mirage of victory, pushed them further towards defeat at the end. Ludendorff was not yet ready for the final stroke in Flanders. He wanted to draw still more French reserves southwards. Also he needed to strengthen and enlarge the flanks of his new salient. At least these were the more or less rational arguments which moved across the surface of his mind. Underneath he was punch drunk, making mechanical gestures of menace like a stunned boxer, and really approaching the point where every thrust weakened his army more than it did the enemy's. Preparations, however, were made on an even greater scale than before – fifty-two German divisions accumulated for an attack east and west of Rheims. This time the Allies were not taken by surprise. Foch guessed right where and when the German attack would come. He called on Haig to take over the defence of more line so as to free French troops for the counter-offensive. It was the turn of the British War Cabinet to be alarmed. They, who had earlier imposed Foch on Haig, now encouraged Haig to defy the supreme commander. Haig refused: though he had little faith in Foch, he had still less in civilian ministers.

The new German offensive came on 15 July. It proved to be the last. The French had been quick to learn from previous failures – not for the first time in the war. East of Rheims their front line was lightly held. It swung back until the Germans were caught between the fire of French machine guns, and decisively halted. West of Rheims the Germans made more progress. This was their nearest advance to Paris. Clemenceau muttered that Foch was losing his grasp. In reality, the opposite had happened. Foch's plans and the actual situation at last coincided. On 18 July the French struck at the exposed flank of the German advance. They had the advantage of morning mist. They mounted a mass attack by tanks on the Cambrai model for the only time in the war. The German line broke. Then there was the old difficulty. The French infantry advanced only four miles before they ran into new obstacles. The German line re-formed. The French had discovered how to make a hole in the enemy line, and the British soon followed them. Neither discovered how to keep this hole open. The German line remained intact until the end of the war.

The German flank was yielding, while their advance units still pushed towards Paris. Ludendorff, confident of success, had already moved north to Mons, where he proposed to give

the order for launching 'Hagen' on 20 July. Instead news came to him of threatening disaster on the Marne. Hastily he gave the order for retreat. The German armies fell back across the Marne, escaping from the French trap. 'Hagen' was called off: theoretically postponed until the Allies had been worn down by a period of German defensive warfare, in fact vanishing from sight for ever. It was the turn of the tide. Four days later, on 24 July, Haig, Pétain, and Pershing came to Foch's head-quarters. The time had come, he told them, for a general offensive. His plan was the old strategy of Joffre, now conducted with better tactics and greater resources. The British were to attack in the extreme north, starting from Ypres; the Americans at the southern end of the line near Verdun. The French armies would keep up a steady pressure in the centre and thus tie down the bulk of the German forces. In this way the entire German army would be encircled.

Events led to victory, but not as Foch had planned. He had to take success as it came, not as he wanted it. The great encirclement would not be ready until the middle of September. Meanwhile Haig designed some local moves to improve his position. His immediate concern was to free the railways east of Amiens. Canadian forces were moved secretly, quite in the

174. French soldiers move cautiously to the offensive, 1918.

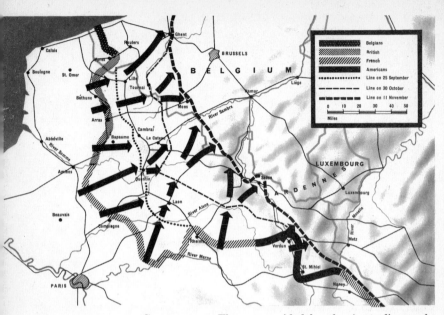

The Allied offensive, 1918

new German way. They were aided by the Australians, who possessed in Sir John Monash the only general of creative originality produced by the First World War. On 8 August the British forces attacked. They had learnt at last the lesson of Cambrai: 456 tanks were used. Thick morning mist played its part. The British advanced a good six miles. Then, as usual, resistance stiffened. The tanks went faster than the cavalry; the infantry lagged behind both. Foch wanted to press the attack in the old frontal way. Haig at first agreed; then was persuaded by his subordinate commanders to stop whenever the enemy proved obstinate. In this accidental way, Foch and Haig stumbled unwillingly on a new and wiser method – to attack at weak points, not at strong ones; they quickly took the credit for it. For the next four weeks there was a succession of Allied attacks, short and sharp: the French Third Army on 10 August; their Tenth Army on 17 August; the British Third Army on 21 August; their First Army on 26 August. In the last of these attacks on 12 September the American army acted independently for the first time and overran the St Mihiel salient, south of Verdun, in less than twenty-four hours.

Ludendorff later called 8 August 'the black day of the German Army'. Not that anything vital was lost from a strategical point of view. Indeed, the month's fighting from

8 August to 12 September nowhere broke the German line. It merely compelled the Germans to abandon the embarrassing salients which they had conquered since 21 March, and they withdrew to stronger defensive positions. Moreover, the Allies, being now once more on the offensive, again suffered the heavier losses. The real effect of 8 August was psychological. It shattered the faith in victory which, until that moment, carried the Germans forward. The German soldiers had been told that they were fighting the decisive battle. Now they realized that the decision had gone against them. They no longer wanted to win. They wanted only to end the war. Even Ludendorff admitted on 15 August that the war would have to be ended by negotiation, not by victory. He still thought that he could wait until 1919. Over on the other side, Foch agreed with him: by mid-September it seemed too late to launch the final campaign.

Still, the great attack started on 26 September. It did not come up to expectations. The vital stroke was to be delivered by the Americans in the Argonne: their advance, it was hoped, would disrupt the entire German system of communications. The Americans had not yet learnt from experience. Pershing followed the old method of attacking the strong points instead

175. British tanks prepare to cross the Hindenburg line.

176. German troops in retreat over the Chemin des Dames, September 1918.

of by-passing them. The troops often waited for the mist to clear instead of welcoming it. As a result they suffered over 100,000 casualties; discipline often broke down; in over a week's fighting they advanced less than eight miles. Further north the British did better and actually got beyond the Hindenburg line. But in Flanders the old obstacle of mud triumphed once more: there was no rolling up of the German flank. The Germans, far from being encircled, were holding on the two flanks and yielding in the centre, thus steadily shortening their line and improving their position.

Yet, all unknown, the great moment had come. On 29 September Ludendorff insisted that there must be an immediate armistice. This was partly because he feared, mistakenly, that the Allies would break through. It was much more because of news from the distant forgotten front at Salonika. In a round-about way this, too, was Ludendorff's doing. Late in 1917, Clemenceau had recalled Sarrail, the 'republican' general, from Salonika. Guillaumat, one of the most admired French leaders, was sent out in his place. He was not allowed to act. In June 1918, when the German attack threatened Paris, Guillaumat was summoned home in case public opinion demanded the dismissal of Pétain. Franchet d'Esperey, one of

177, 178. The American army takes over a sector in the Argonne and joins in the big push.

179. *Marshal Franchet d'Esperey : he advanced from Salonika after all.*

the generals dismissed by Clemenceau, took his place at Salonika. By the time Guillaumat arrived in Paris, the German advance had been stopped. Pétain was safe. Guillaumat found himself with nothing to do. He therefore peddled the claims of his old front at Salonika. He persuaded both Clemenceau and Lloyd George. Franchet d'Esperey was given permission to attack. He did so on 15 September. The Bulgarian army opposing him was badly equipped and weary of war. It yielded almost at the first blow. On 29 September Bulgaria asked for an armistice and withdrew from the war. Southern Europe was wide open. Franchet d'Esperey could advance to the Danube (which he reached on 10 November) and then beyond it. The Salonika offensive did not resolve the long dispute between 'westerners' and 'easterners'. If the army at Salonika had attacked earlier in the war, Ludendorff might have stopped the Balkan hole by moving troops from the Western Front. Now he was too heavily engaged and had none to spare. The war ended when 'western' and 'eastern' strategy combined.

Ludendorff did not envisage unconditional surrender. He imagined, with rather childish cunning, that an armistice would permit the German armies to withdraw from conquered territory, and then to stand on a more formidable defensive position in their own country. The armistice, in Ludendorff's eyes, was a device by which Germany could avoid defeat and emerge from the war undiminished. The civilian ministers objected that the Allies would impose harsh terms on a 'militaristic' Germany. Ludendorff at once produced a solution; there must be a 'revolution from above'. The German people learnt, much to their surprise, that Germany had become a democratic country by order of the High Command. Prince Max of Baden, a prince with a liberal reputation, was appointed Chancellor. Social Democrats joined the Government. Ludendorff and the other generals, of course, regarded all this as window-dressing to deceive the Allies. It was that, and more. Though the revolution started from above, it did not stop there. The German people broke out in a passionate political discussion. The Press was freed. The leftwing opponents of the war could be silenced no longer.

Prince Max was reluctant to ask for an immediate armistice. Unlike Ludendorff, he had the sense to see that the German people would take this as a confession of defeat and would lose the will to fight on. Prince Max would have preferred to negotiate first over possible bases of peace. Ludendorff allowed no delay. His orders were obeyed by the Chancellor for the last

180. Two Bulgarian soldiers set an example to their country by surrendering to the French.

time. On 4 October Germany formally requested an armistice. Prince Max got part of his way. The German note was addressed to President Wilson, not to Foch, the Allied Commander-in-Chief; and it accepted Wilson's Fourteen Points and subsequent pronouncements as the basis for peace negotiations. This was an adroit move. It put the Germans on the same idealistic level as Wilson. It put them ahead of the Allies, who had never accepted the Fourteen Points. Nor, for that matter, had the American people, many of whom wanted total and punitive victory. Wilson still hoped for a peace without victors or vanquished. He still regretted that he was head of a belligerent nation, not a detached mediator. Now Prince Max was offering to become Wilson's ally against the Allies, against fire-eating Americans and – to some extent – against Wilson himself. Wilson saw the chance of turning the war into an idealistic crusade after all. He did not consult the Allies. Instead he ignored their protests and warnings. He replied directly to Prince Max on 8 October. As though unable to believe his luck, he asked whether Germany really accepted the Fourteen Points? Had she genuinely satisfied his further requirements of making the world safe for democracy and become a democratic country? Wilson added, as a sop to the Allies, that the Germans must evacuate all occupied territory before he could promote an armistice on their behalf. He could hardly demand less. It seemed as though Prince Max's calculations were coming true: Germany was being offered a harmless, innocent peace merely at the price of withdrawing within her own frontiers.

The European Allies were alarmed: they feared that they were being cheated of the fruits of victory at the last moment. The Germans were correspondingly delighted. On 12 October Prince Max replied enthusiastically to Wilson: Germany, he repeated, accepted the Fourteen Points. He speculated, tellingly, whether the Allies did the same. Fortune did not favour Prince Max. On 12 October a German submarine sank the *Leinster*, a ship running between England and Ireland. 450 passengers were drowned, some of them American. This was the very German 'barbarism' which had drawn America into the war – or so most Americans liked to think. Wilson himself was offended. On 16 October he replied to the Germans in firmer tones. Submarine warfare must stop at once; an armistice, as distinct from peace negotiations, must be settled by the military commanders; and Germany must produce clearer, more convincing evidence that she had become a democratic state. Prince Max realized that he had not been so clever after all: the Fourteen Points really meant something; Wilson's idealism was not merely hot air.

On 17 October the rulers of Germany, old and new, debated what to do: democratic ministers on one side, Ludendorff and the High Command on the other. Ludendorff had recovered from his fright of a fortnight before. He was now all for fighting on. Maybe he wanted to shift the blame on to the civilian ministers. The military situation was also more favourable. The great Allied attack was running down. The German army was being neither encircled nor broken. Ludendorff saw through a haze the prospect of continuing a defensive war in 1919. By then the situation might change in some unforeseeable way – France might collapse, Great Britain and America might quarrel. Prince Max rejected this dreamy gambling. The German generals and admirals were overruled – for the first time in Germany during the war, and a rare event in any country. Unrestricted submarine warfare was called off unconditionally. Wilson's condition of a military armistice was accepted on 20 October. With this went assurances that Germany had become truly liberal. Indeed she had. The rejection of Ludendorff's policy was evidence for this. Few

181. President Wilson (extreme left) and his Cabinet prepare to rule the world.

Germans appreciated the legend of Imperialist Germany which had grown up in Allied countries, nor the absurd bitterness against 'the Kaiser'. They imagined that they had atoned for all the events of the war by becoming democratic on Wilson's instruction; and Wilson's own attitude gave them some excuse. Even those Germans who had read the Fourteen Points noticed only the generalities – the references to the League of Nations and to reconciliation between peoples. It did not occur to them that Germany would have to surrender territory to Poland, still less that they would still be treated as 'the enemy'. Prince Max and those associated with him imagined that they had become Wilson's allies. Wilson however took a onesided view of this alliance just as he did of his relationship with the Allies. He was free to play fast-and-loose. Others were not.

On 23 October Wilson announced himself satisfied with the German answer. He now asked the generals to draft an armistice and, at the same time, invited the Allies to accept the Fourteen Points as basis for the future peace. This was a strange way for the war to end. The United States, which had borne least of the burden and done least of the fighting, dictated terms to Allies and enemies alike. Of course the United States were the strongest Power in the world. But this was not the main reason for Wilson's authority. The Allies had never managed to formulate any war aims in regard to Germany except victory. Secretly the French hoped to carry off the Rhineland, the British to acquire the German colonies. They had reached no agreement on this, and had fallen back on idealistic phrases – a war to end war, or to make the world safe for democracy. They were now caught by their own phrases.

The armistice was intended to be purely a military agreement, which would end the fighting and ensure that Germany could not renew it later on more favourable terms. Inevitably, therefore, it was stern. In this way Ludendorff, by insisting on an armistice instead of on negotiations for peace, brought down on Germany the defeat which he had intended to avoid. Haig believed that the Germans had still plenty of resistance left in them, and he would have been content if they withdrew from all occupied territory. Pershing, at the other extreme, acted in complete contradiction with Wilson, his political chief, and wanted no armistice at all, in order to give his relatively untried army a chance of further success. Foch claimed to judge in military terms. Actually he was determined to get the

Rhineland for France whatever the Fourteen Points said, and therefore smuggled occupation of the Rhineland into the armistice ostensibly on grounds of security. The British Admiralty insisted that the entire German fleet must be handed over, or at any rate interned. Foch attached no importance to the war at sea, quite mistakenly. But he struck a bargain with the British admirals, who then supported him against Haig's moderate terms. The British got the German navy; Foch got the Rhineland. The Allies thought it beyond their strength to demand the dissolution of the German army. Besides, they were already alarmed at the spectre of 'Bolshevism'. The Germans were therefore merely to hand over a large part of their fighting material.

Meanwhile the political leaders debated whether to accept the Fourteen Points. After a few kicks of independence, they decided that the Fourteen Points were not really objectionable after all. Lloyd George refused to accept the freedom of the seas – in any case a peculiarly odd demand for Wilson to make when the United States were enforcing the blockade far more ruthlessly than ever the British had done. As an American admiral said to Balfour in 1917: 'You will find that it will take us only two months to become as great criminals as you are!' Lloyd George and Clemenceau also insisted that Germany must pay for the damage caused to civilians and to their property in Allied countries. No one then foresaw the weary tangle over reparations to which this would lead. The Italian representative tried to challenge the Point which laid down that Italy should only acquire territory inhabited by Italians. He was brusquely told that they were discussing solely the terms with Germany, and was battered into silence. Thus the way was left open for the bitterest wrangle of the peace conference. At the time, Wilson thought he had won. Peace would be made on the idealistic terms which he had devised; a new world would be created, free from war and safe for democracy.

At the very moment of triumph, Wilson's position crumbled behind him. His opponents, the Republicans, won the elections to Congress. The American people repudiated Wilson's programme. They did not want the United States to be embedded in an idealistic peace. They wanted only to defeat Germany and then to turn their backs on the world once more. The German position was crumbling also. On the Western Front, they were still holding their own. Though they fell back, their defensive line remained unbroken. Devastation,

182. The Emir Feisal learns that he is not to rule in Damascus.

lack of communications, and nests of machine gunners held up the Allied advance. It was otherwise with the German rear. Germany's allies collapsed. The Ottoman Empire was the first to dissolve. One British army under Allenby reached Damascus on 1 October. Another was moving up the Euphrates to the oil wells of Mosul. On 30 October Turkey signed an armistice of surrender with a British admiral, much to the annoyance of Clemenceau who thought that France also ought to have been represented. The British navy steamed belatedly through the Dardanelles. Constantinople passed under Allied control. The Allies were free to advance up the Danube against Germany. They were also free to intervene against the Bolsheviks in southern Russia – a freedom of which they foolishly took advantage. Though the Sultan remained as a virtual prisoner in Allied hands, the Ottoman Empire was at an end.

The Habsburg Empire vanished at almost the same moment. The two old enemies, and in the last years allies, went down together into the limbo of forgotten things. Austria-Hungary had been rocking on her feet throughout 1918. In mid-June the Habsburg army in Italy undertook a last futile offensive which achieved some success against an Italian army that was even shakier. Then the fighting spirit of both armies ran out. Italians

183. They are there because they are there : British troops enter Damascus.

and Austrians clashed mechanically in a common hopelessness. As with Germany, it was the attempt to escape defeat by negotiations which brought Austria-Hungary to final disaster. The Austro-Hungarian Government, like the German, asked President Wilson to arrange peace on the basis of the Fourteen Points. Wilson could not do so. The Fourteen Points had assumed the survival of the Habsburg Monarchy with 'autonomy' for its various nationalities. Since announcing them, Wilson had promised independence to the Czechs and Poles, less formally to the Rumanians and South Slavs. He therefore replied that these nations, and not he, must decide on the peace terms. This was the signal for revolt. The so-called 'subject' nationalities of Austria-Hungary learnt that they could escape the burden of defeat and become Allies merely by transforming themselves into independent nations. Naturally they did so. The revolutions were of a harmless kind. In Prague the Imperial Governor rang the secret number of the Czech National Committee which he had known all along. They came round to the Castle. The Governor handed over his seals and keys. Then he left. The civil servants remained at their desks. Ten minutes of conversation had created Czechoslovakia as an independent country.

184. End of an empire: symbols of Habsburg authority torn down in Prague.

Much the same happened with the South Slav Committee at Zagreb. The Croats and Slovenes woke up subjects of the Habsburg Emperor Charles, and went to bed as subjects, along with the Serbs, of King Peter Karageorgevich. In Vienna Count Bilinski, last Austro-Hungarian Minister of Finance, locked his office and took the train for Warsaw, where he became first Polish Minister of Finance without losing a day of his pension rights. Nor was it only the 'subject' nationalities who abandoned the Habsburgs. The Hungarians tried, rather unconvincingly, to turn themselves into an oppressed people. Michael Karolyi, a sincere opponent of the war, became Prime Minister, on 31 October. Two days later he proclaimed the independence of Hungary and became Hungary's first President. The Germans of Vienna were the last to leave the sinking ship, but only because the sinking ship refused to leave them. Emperor Charles was still at Vienna on 12 November, when his German lands proclaimed themselves part of the future German democratic state. Not all this ingenuity was rewarded. The Czechs, the South Slavs, the Poles, duly became Allies, as did the Rumanians by denouncing their peace treaty with Germany and re-entering the war one day before it ended. The Hungarians and German Austrians were not so

185. The triumph of his determination: Masaryk returns to Prague as President of Czechoslovakia, 1918.

lucky. Though they had fought the war no more, and no less, than the other nationalities, they alone were treated as heirs of the dead Empire and saddled with its guilt. They were compulsorily disarmed, charged theoretically with reparations. This was a strange distinction. Democratic Hungary and republican Austria paid a penalty for retaining their former imperial names.

The Austro-Hungarian army actually outlived the state which it had been created to defend. Only on 23 October did the Italians nerve themselves to attack, and even then the most successful advance was by the British army corps under Lord Cavan. The news from home brought the Austro-Hungarian army to an end. Why should men go on fighting for an Empire which no longer existed? The soldiers deserted in whole regiments, finding their way back to their own countries as best they could. On 2 November the new Hungarian Republic formally recalled all Hungarian troops. The Austro-Hungarian High Command sought an armistice in hasty desperation. The armistice was signed on 3 November. It was to come into force twenty-four hours later. During this period the Habsburg army ceased to exist. The Italians, advancing at last, took three hundred thousand unresisting prisoners. This is known in the books as the battle of Vittorio Veneto. As a last stroke of independence, the Austro-Hungarian navy at Pola was handed over to the Yugoslav National Council, in the hope of saving it from the Italians.

The German rear was thus wide open, the Allied armies preparing to advance into southern Germany. The final stroke came in Germany itself. On 26 October William II, quite forgetting that he was now a constitutional monarch, dismissed Ludendorff on his own impulse. Three days later, William left Berlin for army headquarters, still confident of a long, successful defensive. The Government urged him to return. He defied them. Defiance came also from the German admirals. They were indignant at having to call off submarine warfare. They resolved to send the High Seas Fleet into action against the British, perhaps in the hope of wrecking the armistice negotiations, perhaps in the belief that they (or rather the men on board ship) preferred death to dishonour. Secret orders were hastily issued to raise steam and prepare for battle. The sailors had not been in action for more than two years; during that time they had hardly been at sea. An army will keep going, even when defeated, while it is in contact with the enemy. It

186, 187, 188. Revolution in Germany.

was different with sailors who had been living quietly with their families. On 29 October the crews began to mutiny. Two days later they went ashore and carried the mutiny through the streets of Kiel. By 3 November Kiel was in their hands. It was the beginning of the German revolution. Soon the news reached Berlin. Prince Max and his colleagues were convinced that revolution would soon spread throughout Germany. They were resolved now to bring the war to an end – no longer to avert defeat, but to prevent revolution.

Erzberger, leading figure of the Centre, was put at the head of the Armistice Commission. The Commission, unlike most such, did not include any representative of the High Command. This omission is often explained as a deliberate trick to relieve the High Command of all blame for defeat. As a matter of fact, it was done from fear that a military representative might raise difficulties and so prolong the war. On 7 November Erzberger asked, by wireless, for a meeting with Foch. He crossed the fighting line that evening when it was already dark. He and the other delegates were driven through the night. At eight o'clock the next morning they met Foch and Admiral Wemyss, the supreme naval spokesman, in a railway carriage at Rethondes in the forest of Compiègne. Erzberger asked for an armistice. Foch read out the terms on which the Allies had agreed. In Paris there was some doubt whether the Germans would accept terms so harsh. Events made the German Government grasp at an armistice on almost any terms. On 9 November the revolution finally took fire. A republic was proclaimed in Berlin. Prince Max handed over his position as Chancellor to Ebert, leader of the Social Democrats. At Spa, the army headquarters, the generals told William II that the armies would fight perhaps for Germany, but not for the Emperor. William retired to his special train, and steamed away early the next morning. Then he changed over to a car that was secretly waiting, and drove to the Dutch frontier. He was allowed to cross after some hours' delay. Two days later he signed his formal abdication as King of Prussia and German Emperor. He never saw Germany again, though the income from his vast German properties continued to roll in until his death in 1941.

The new republican government in Berlin were too busy staving off revolution to waste time discussing the armistice terms. Erzberger received brief instructions to sign at once. In a last meeting with Foch he bargained, not unsuccessfully.

The German army was allowed to keep some of its machine guns – perhaps for use against the so-called internal enemy, Bolshevism. Erzberger did not win his most urgent point, a relaxation of the blockade. After signing the armistice at 5 a.m. on 11 November, he handed over a declaration which ended: 'A nation of seventy millions of people suffers, but it does not die.' Foch replied: 'Très bien', and withdrew without shaking hands. At 11 a.m. that morning the fighting stopped. The war was over. The German army, still unbroken, stood everywhere on foreign soil, except for a few villages which the French had held throughout the war in Alsace. Canadian troops entered Mons an hour before the armistice came into force. The British army was back where it started.

By the armistice the Germans were to hand over vast stocks of war material and most of their fleet. They were to withdraw from all invaded territory in the west and from Alsace Lorraine. The Allied armies were to occupy German territory on the left bank of the Rhine, and the bridgeheads for fifty miles beyond it. The treaties of Brest Litovsk and Bucarest were annulled. This was the crushing victory to which the Allies had aspired, though by no means the destruction of the German army, still less the dismemberment of the German *Reich*. The German

189. Marshal Foch obligingly signs the armistice by the carriage window.

190, 191. 'Now this bleeding war is over, no more soldiering for me.'

revolution was not the cause of defeat. On the contrary, the revolution was caused by Ludendorff's confession that the war was lost. More than this, the revolution saved both the German army and German unity. The armistice came when Germany still held together. The Allies themselves had to desire a strong German government if the armistice were to be maintained or a peace treaty signed. Future victory was snatched by the Germans from present defeat.

On 11 November 1918 the Allied peoples burst into rejoicing. All work stopped for the day. Crowds blocked the streets, dancing and cheering. In Trafalgar Square Canadian soldiers lit a bonfire at the plinth of Nelson's column, the marks of which can be seen to this day. As evening fell, the crowds grew more riotous. Total strangers copulated in public – a symbol that life had triumphed over death. The celebrations went on for two more days, becoming increasingly destructive. In the end the police cleared the streets. Things were quieter in Paris after the first day. The death roll of the French was too great to be forgotten even in victory. Far off in Moscow, the news of Germany's defeat was received with sombre triumph. The Supreme Soviet formally repudiated the treaty of Brest Litovsk. Lenin had been vindicated, though not thanks to the

192. *Armistice Day celebrations in Paris.*

international proletariat. Now, however, the Bolsheviks imagined that revolution would sweep across Europe in a matter of days. Communism, they believed, was on the threshold of a victorious career. Many in the West feared the same thing.

What happened on 11 November 1918? Merely the military defeat of Germany? Or the triumph of idealistic principles, enshrined in the Fourteen Points? The peoples now had to answer these questions. Perhaps the contrast is too sharp. Germany was universally regarded in Allied countries as the aggressor and the barbarian. Hence harshness towards Germany seemed compatible with the highest ideals. It was obvious to the French that their victory meant the victory of civilization, and anything which strengthened this victory made civilization more secure. Lloyd George in Great Britain looked forward to a peace of conciliation. This, of course, was only possible if he remained in power. The existing parliament was eight years old. It had long outlived its welcome. There was an immediate general election. All parties talked of a new world free from war. All talked too of punishing the Kaiser and of making Germany pay. Lloyd George had grave doubts whether defeated and ruined Germany could pay much, if indeed anything.

But he needed votes. He announced in ringing tones: 'I will make the Germans pay.' Then added softly, during the applause: ' . . . as much as they can.' Similarly, he acquiesced in the outcry against 'war criminals'. As an experienced solicitor, he disliked going to court on any issue. It was a Labour leader, not Lloyd George, who proclaimed: 'I am for hanging the Kaiser' (trial and hanging being regarded as synonymous). The aristocratic Lord Curzon and Lord Birkenhead, the Lord Chancellor, forced the project through. The election which had been intended to clear the way for a better world ended with all parties, except a few opponents of the war, exclaiming: 'Hang the Kaiser! Make Germany pay!'

A disaster for idealism and high principles, or so it seemed. Yet perhaps not. If the Allies had been fighting for high ideals and the Germans for wicked ones, then surely it was right that the Germans should pay for the war and that their leaders should be punished. A peace of reconciliation could be preached only by those who held that there was nothing to choose between the two sides and that the only fault of the Germans was to have lost. Who dared say that at the time? How many, outside Germany, would say it now? In the age of mass warfare, nations had to be told that they were fighting for some noble cause. Perhaps they were. At any rate, the peoples could not be told to forget their crusading beliefs merely because the war was over. The statesmen who had won the war had to make peace with the same emotions and the same weapons.

·194. *President Wilson about to lay a fifteenth point.*

Afterwards: **1919**

The Great War was over. Little wars went on. Throughout eastern Europe, the new states were hastily organizing armies of their own; setting up frontier posts; disputing with their neighbours over territory. No one knew what was to happen to the abandoned lands of the Ottoman Empire, now mostly under British military control. There were still armies of intervention in Russia: Japanese in Siberia, British at Archangel and Murmansk, French in the south, German forces in the Baltic which the Allies hesitated to order out. No one could decide whether to negotiate with the Bolsheviks, to intervene massively against them, or to wait passively for their expected collapse. The victorious Allies and the United States, their associate, seemed to dominate the world. Their military power was a wasting asset. The soldiers of every nation wanted to go home. There were mutinies in the American camps in France; mutinies in the British camp at Folkestone, which were quietened only by the intervention of Horatio Bottomley. One body of British troops marched from Victoria Station to the Horse Guards Parade, where they demonstrated against the Secretary for War, Winston Churchill. Canadian soldiers mutinied at Rhyl, and were brought to order only after six of them had been killed. The economic power of the victors was a wasting asset also. The peoples of Europe wanted food and financial assistance. The Allies had little to give. They were hard enough pressed keeping things going in their own countries. American loans stopped abruptly with the armistice. The systems of Allied cooperation over finance and transport were ended on American insistence. The Allies were not strong enough to make a new world. The world was left to make itself.

Peace was the immediate need. On 18 January 1919 the Peace Conference assembled at Paris. President Wilson came in person, the first President to leave the United States during his term of office. Peace had always been his speciality, and he could not leave its making to anyone else. As a result, the heads of other states had to come too. Clemenceau was on the spot. Lloyd George moved most of the British Government from London to Paris. Premier Orlando came from Italy. At first there was an attempt at more or less formal discussion in the Council of Ten – two delegates from each Great Power (Great

Britain, France, Italy, Japan, and the United States). When
negotiations jammed, the great men brushed the Council of
Ten aside and set themselves up as the Big Four – really three,
Lloyd George, Clemenceau, and Wilson, with Orlando occasionally voicing Italy's interest. These three men had to make the
peace settlement. They were overworked and tired, distracted
by affairs in their own countries and constantly breaking off
their long-term deliberations to settle some immediate question.
No meeting of the Big Four ever managed to concentrate on
a single topic. Discussion was for ever hopping from one question to another. Only Clemenceau understood both French and
English. Everything therefore had to be translated by Professor
Mantoux. The Big Four were not only peacemakers. They were
also the Supreme Council of the Allies, issuing orders for immediate action. Wilson had to go home for a month during the
meeting of Congress. Lloyd George went to London more than
once in order to silence complaints in the House of Commons.
He travelled always by rail and sea, a full day's journey. Only
Bonar Law, his colleague, was adventurous enough to come to
Paris by air. Orlando was often pulled back to Rome. Clemenceau, though safe from these distractions, was also removed

from activity when a nationalist fanatic shot and severely wounded him. The work of the Big Four has been much criticized. Perhaps it is a wonder they managed to settle anything.

The statesmen were expected to build the peace of the world on idealistic foundations; yet at the same time to satisfy the bitter resentments which had accumulated during the war and to promote the interests of their respective countries. Wilson arrived in Europe with the firm conviction that all statesmen were wicked except himself. He had outmanoeuvred the wicked once when he compelled them to accept the Fourteen Points. He intended to do it again by compelling them to accept the League of Nations, his solution for all ills. This turned out to be easier than he had expected. The European Allies, too, wanted a League of Nations, though not quite on Wilson's pattern. The British had prepared a detailed scheme, which was more than Wilson had done. It suited his outlook well enough, and he adopted most of it. This 'Anglo-Saxon' League relied on influence, or at most on moral force. Its members would meet, discuss, and conciliate. Any restless Power would be tamed by a threat of disapproval from the others. The French produced a scheme of a different character: a League to maintain peace (particularly against Germany) by armed might,

196. President Wilson resolves that to preserve his impartiality he will not visit Rheims again.

little more in fact than the war indefinitely prolonged into peace-time. There was an ironical outcome. Wilson, who had expected to have to push the League down the Allies' throats, instead spent his time resisting their attempts to make the League a reality. It was particularly embarrassing for him when the Japanese maliciously tried to write the principle of race equality into the League Covenant. Wilson had to buy them off by presenting them with Shantung, the former German sphere in China. Still, he got the League settled before anything else. It was to be embedded in the peace treaty with Germany, though Germany, oddly enough, was not to be a member – at any rate not until she had demonstrated her democratic and pacific character. Once Wilson got the League, he cared less about other questions. Details of the settlement that were at fault could, he supposed, be put right once the League started to function.

The British, too, obtained most of what they wanted before the practical discussion began, though on topics different from Wilson's. Their prime object throughout had been the destruction of the German fleet. With this fleet interned at Scapa Flow (failing any neutral port willing to receive it), this object was as good as accomplished. The British Government also

197. Admiral Beatty has won the war.

198, 199, *The German battle fleet surrenders.*

200. *Victims of the blockade: German children receive food from a street kitchen.*

201. *An un-defeated army: German soldiers return to Berlin after being stabbed in the back.*

wanted to lay hands on the German colonies, for reasons which remain obscure – probably habit from previous wars. The British Dominions had more immediate motives for the same demand. South Africa wanted German South West Africa. Australia wanted New Guinea. Lloyd George took a malicious pleasure in hearing Wilson defied by the Australian, Hughes, and the South African, Smuts – spokesmen allegedly of a democratic idealism uncorrupted by contact with the old world. Wilson said to Hughes: 'Is Australia prepared to defy the appeal of the whole civilized world?' Hughes adjusted his hearing aid (he was very deaf), and replied cheerfully: 'That's about the size of it, President Wilson.' 'Mandates' had to be invented hastily in order to conceal the Imperialist greed of the Dominions; and the British Government added its own quota of disguised annexation in East Africa, so as to keep things respectable. The German colonies were of little value. Still, this was not a particularly creditable transaction. One could trust Smuts, the great operator of fraudulent idealism, to be mixed up in it.

The great practical effect was that both the United States and Great Britain came to the actual peace negotiations with Germany in an almost detached frame of mind. The original intention had been that the Allies should settle among themselves what they wanted, and should then negotiate with the Germans, to see how far they could get it. This scheme did not work out. The victors faced an awkward and increasingly difficult problem. The military superiority of the Allies had compelled the Germans to sue for an armistice. Now this superiority was wasting away by demobilization with every day which passed. If negotiations dragged on long enough, the Germans might reappear as equals, not as the defeated. The Allies had one remaining weapon – the blockade against Germany which was still being enforced. It seemed a barbaric weapon now that fighting was over. British forces in the Rhineland, from the commanding general downwards, protested against the blockade, and shared their food with hungry women and children. The blockade had to be ended before peace was signed. It was suggested as a compromise that a preliminary peace should be made, containing only the military terms, so that Germany would be effectively disarmed. American objections killed this proposal. Even a preliminary peace would have to be submitted to the American Senate for ratification; and Wilson knew that he would have difficulty enough in getting this once, let alone twice. Besides, Wilson, with the complacency of a true idealist, held that any peace which satisfied him must obviously be beyond criticism and that there was no need to wait for arguments from the Germans. He would know what was best for them as for everyone else. Thus, thanks to Wilson's high principles, the democratic and idealistic Powers surpassed even the behaviour of the Germans at Brest Litovsk, where the Bolsheviks had at least been allowed to argue round the table, and imposed peace by dictation, with hardly a pretence of negotiation.

The Germans had expected something much more generous than the treatment of Brest Litovsk, not much less. They had supposed that Germany, too, would be accepted as a peaceful, democratic Power, once the Kaiser was got rid of and the fighting brought to an end. There would be a peace without victors or vanquished. This did not happen. The Allied peoples had been told during the war that there was nothing to choose between Germans. They remembered that the German Socialists, now heading the Government, had supported the war until it ended in defeat. Only a handful of leftwing Germans thought that German policy had been wicked; and they were the associates of Allied leftwingers who were most bitterly denounced in their own countries as pacifists or traitors. If Lloyd George or Clemenceau once admitted that there were any 'good Germans', then they condemned their own policy of the knock-out blow and confessed that Ramsay MacDonald or even Lenin had been right after all. Hence there was no such reconciliation as there had been after the Great War a century previously, when the Allies made out that they had been fighting only Napoleon, not France. It was easier for despotic monarchs to forget their hatreds than for democratic statesmen or peoples. The Germans felt that they had been cheated: first in having peace dictated to them; then in being treated as enemies.

In the last resort, after laborious months, security, reparation, justice, all tangled together. As security, Germany was disarmed: no air force, virtually no navy, no tanks, no heavy guns, and a control commission to see that this was enforced. The French wanted to limit the German army to 200,000 conscripts. The British and Americans, shocked at the very word 'conscription', insisted on a limit of 100,000 long-service volunteers, who became the training officers of a new army later. The Anglo-Saxons, somewhat ashamed of this one-sided disarmament, slipped in a clause that it was designed in order to make disarmament easier for others. This clause, though not a binding promise, had awkward consequences later on. The victor Powers found themselves pushed into the Disarmament Conference. The disarmament arrangements, though often criticized later, worked while they lasted. Germany was genuinely disarmed, as near as makes no difference. The victors enjoyed fifteen years of real security. No treaty, after all, can provide that it will be enforced when those who benefit from it are too supine to enforce it.

The French were not content with the disarmament of Germany. They wished to detach the left bank of the Rhine from Germany and to set it up as an independent state, or rather as a state dependent on themselves. Among the few German protagonists of this scheme was Konrad Adenauer, the mayor of Cologne. Lloyd George resisted it firmly. He looked forward to a time when men, including himself, would come to their senses, and was determined that reconciliation with Germany should not be made impossible. He was prepared to accept temporary terms of inequality: the Rhineland to be made a neutral zone and to be occupied by Allied troops for fifteen years; the Saar valley, with its coal mines, to be in

202. The strong hand which lost its grip: occupation of the Ruhr, 1923.

203. There was mud in the east too: Poland at the end of the war.

French hands for the same period, to compensate for the mines in north-east France which had been wilfully wrecked by the Germans. These terms would pass. Germany would emerge free and united. A separate Rhineland would offend against the self-determination in which they all claimed to believe. Lloyd George silenced the French cry for security by proposing instead an Anglo-American guarantee of France against German aggression. Clemenceau accepted the offer, only to be defrauded when the American Senate failed to ratify the treaty of guarantee. German territory in the west remained intact except for the return of Alsace and Lorraine to France, and a couple of villages added to Belgium.

On the eastern frontier of Germany, Lloyd George had a more difficult time. Wilson, or maybe Wilson's expert advisers, sympathized with the new Poland, and were lavish with what had been German territory. The French, too, were of course strong on the same side. Lloyd George, so often despised as unprincipled, was the one man who stuck to his principles. He insisted on a plebiscite in Silesia, which turned out in Germany's favour (too much so from the point of national division). He held out firmly against the incorporation into Poland of Danzig, a purely German town. Thanks to Lloyd George, Danzig became a Free City – politically independent, though economically available for Poland. Thus the arrangement which ostensibly provoked Germany into starting the Second World War was actually designed for her benefit. It is hard to find fault with the new frontiers of Germany drawn at Paris from the standpoint of self determination. This was a 'fair' settlement if there can be such a thing. There was one negative offence against principle. The German inhabitants of rump Austria wished to join Germany now that the Habsburg Empire had vanished; and there could be no clearer case for national unification. The French objected that the war would have been fought in vain and victory would be a mockery, if Germany came out of the war with more inhabitants than when she went in. The argument was accepted. Union of Austria with Germany was forbidden except with the consent of the future League of Nations. The French argument was reasonable enough. However the Germans managed to acquire at least one Austrian without anyone's consent. He was Adolf Hitler. Perhaps it would have been better if they had acquired the other six million Austrians also.

Reparations caused most fuss during the negotiations, and

204. Corporal Hitler (right) and friends.

205. *Corporal
Hitler and another
friend.*

came in for most blame later. It was of course absurd to expect
that Germany could be made to pay all the costs of the war,
though the statesmen, from Lloyd George downwards, shrank
from explaining publicly how absurd it was. All the same, there
was excuse for the difficulties which the statesmen got into. It
seemed reasonable enough that the Germans, whose own
country had not suffered at all, should repair the damage which
they had caused in Belgium and northern France. This was
awkward for Great Britain, which had also suffered little
damage, and would therefore get little reparation. She claimed
German ships, in compensation for those which the U-boats
had sunk, only to discover that this put her own shipyards out
of work. The idealist Smuts was ready, as usual, with a way
out: he suggested that war pensions were also a civil damage,
and thus the British got their share after all. The French
wanted to draw up a bill for the total damage, and present it
to the Germans, even though it would be beyond their capacity
to pay. Wilson, on the other hand, wanted to fix Germany's
capacity, which would be much less than the French claim.
Lloyd George realized that any such total would be wildly
inflated in the excited conditions of the time, an excitement
which his own financial experts shared. He proposed that

reparations should be settled in quieter days later. He got his way. Germany had to recognize full liability – the so-called 'war guilt' clause; her actual payments were left to an expert commission. Nothing caused so much ill-feeling in the inter-war years as the wrangles over reparations. Yet the question had been left open in the interests of reconciliation and good sense. Unfortunately, these took longer to operate than Lloyd George had hoped; and when they did they were out of date.

Such, at any rate, was the treaty presented to the Germans in May 1919. They were allowed to make objections in writing; and they received some concessions on Lloyd George's urging, principally the plebiscite in Silesia. In mid-June they were faced with an ultimatum: they must sign the treaty without further amendment, or the war would be renewed. There was bitter debate in the German National Assembly which was meeting at Weimar to draw up a constitution for the German Republic. Ebert, now President, consulted Hindenburg by telephone. Hindenburg said to Groener, his assistant who had succeeded Ludendorff: 'You know what the answer must be. I am going for a walk.' When the telephone rang again, Groener gave the answer: 'The army could hold its own against the Poles in the east. It could not resist an Allied advance in the west.' This answer determined the majority of the Assembly to accept the treaty. When Hindenburg came in from his walk, he laid his hand on Groener's shoulder and said: 'You have taken upon yourself a heavy responsibility.' This was by no means the only occasion when Germans in high places avoided blame for what was happening. Though the Germans accepted the treaty in the formal sense of agreeing to sign it, none of them took the signature seriously. The treaty seemed to them wicked, unfair, dictation, a slave treaty. All Germans intended to repudiate the treaty at some time in the future, if it did not first fall to pieces of its own absurdity.

The news of the German agreement was received in Paris with rejoicing. The threat to renew the war was a bluff which succeeded. No one knew whether the Allies had enough armed forces with which to march into Germany, still less whether the forces would march. These speculations were now un-necessary. The victory of November 1918 still had its prestige. This prestige was exploited to the limit. The formal signing of the treaty was arranged in the Hall of Mirrors at Versailles, where the German Empire had been proclaimed in 1871. On 28 June 1919, the fashionable population of Paris and the

newspapermen of all the world streamed to Versailles. The
Germans were brought in as though under armed guard. They
signed. The victors signed. The fountains played. Guns fired in
rejoicing. The First World War was over.

Much more tidying up remained to be done, some of it never
accomplished. Though the peace settlement of 1919 is often
described generally as 'Versailles', the treaty signed on 28
June related only to Germany. There were other peace treaties
distributed round Paris, until the stock of adjacent palaces was
almost exhausted. Neuilly with Bulgaria, and St Germain with
Austria in 1919; Trianon with Hungary, and Sèvres with
Turkey in 1920. These are the treaties usually denounced under
the heading of 'Versailles'. The treaties which are supposed to
have 'balkanized' Europe and to have cleared the way for a
Second World War. In reality the peacemakers, from the Big
Four downwards, had relatively little to do with these treaties,
which for the most part made themselves. The new national
states, so much condemned by those who have always enjoyed
national freedom, were not the creation of Versailles or even,
more correctly, of Paris. They were already in full existence
before the Peace Conference assembled. They were sovereign
states, most of them Allies. The Big Four could not have

*206. Ledebour,
left-wing Socialist,
attacks the German
government.*

imposed disarmament or free trade on these states, even if they had wanted to do so. The Peace Conference could settle some details of the various frontiers, no more. Bulgaria was the only one which had a real continuity with the old state of the same name. Austria, Hungary, and Turkey were as much new states as Czechoslovakia, Rumania, or Yugoslavia, though they were treated as enemies. The so-called enemy states usually lost when a frontier was in dispute; and they were saddled with imaginary reparations, though, far from paying these, they soon had to be financially sustained by the former victors. Self determination, on national lines, did not work out as simply as President Wilson had once expected. Nationalities were mixed up; often the real national allegiance could not be discovered even by a plebiscite. Ingenious lines of national division cut across railway lines and areas economically tied together. The Germans of Czechoslovakia, though indignant at being put 'under' the Czechs, were even more indignant at the suggestion that they should be separated from the 'natural' unit of Bohemia, to which they had belonged for almost as long as the Czechs themselves. The frontiers were not perfect even from the national point of view. Still, fewer people were under an alien national sovereignty than ever before in European history; and the frontiers so abruptly drawn in 1919 and 1920 have survived almost without change except as between Poland and Germany, to the present day.

Peace conferences rarely concentrate on the great questions which seem to deserve their attention. They are usually distracted by some topic which has little significance for later generations. So it was with the Conference of 1919. Maybe the great men ought to have been busy, healing the scars of war and building a better world. Much of their time was in fact taken up with the question: should Italy or Yugoslavia, the new state of the South Slavs, have the town of Fiume? The Italians had the asset of being a Great Power; the Yugoslavs that President Wilson thought their claim was just. Here, it seemed to him, was the old conflict between Right and Might; and he was determined that Right should win. He held up all other proceedings while this dispute was repeatedly debated, and appealed to the morality of the Italian people over the heads of their rulers – only to encounter a fierce shout of national hostility. The Peace Conference never settled the question of Fiume. Italy and Yugoslavia were left to negotiate on their own. Yugoslavia, the weaker, was driven to give way.

207. German
delegates sign the
Treaty of
Versailles.

208. He set an
example which
Mussolini
followed: Gabriele
D'Annunzio at
Fiume.

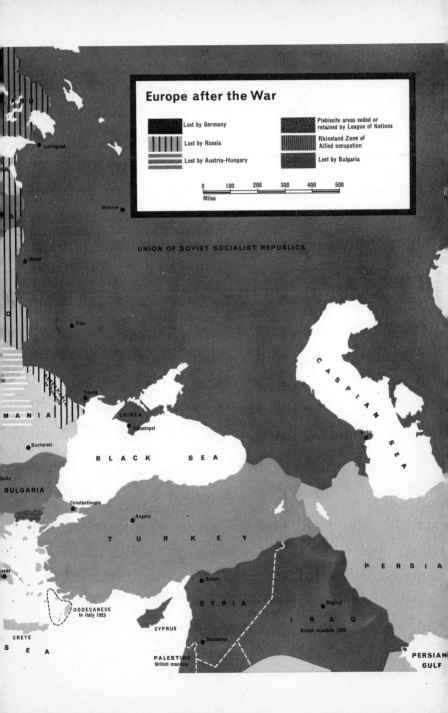

Europe after the War

Lost by Germany

Lost by Russia

Lost by Austria-Hungary

Plebiscite areas ceded or retained by League of Nations

Rhineland Zone of Allied occupation

Lost by Bulgaria

0   100   200   300   400   500
Miles

Leningrad

Moscow

UNION OF SOVIET SOCIALIST REPUBLICS

Minsk

Kiev

CASPIAN SEA

Odessa

RUMANIA

CRIMEA

Sebastopol

Baku

BLACK   SEA

Bucharest

Sofia

BULGARIA

Constantinople

Angora

TURKEY

PERSIA

Aleppo

DODECANESE
to Italy 1923

SYRIA

CYPRUS

IRAQ

Bagdad

British mandate 1920

CRETE

SEA

Damascus

PALESTINE
British mandate

PERSIAN
GULF

Fiume became a Free City in 1920. Italy annexed it in 1924, only to lose it after the Second World War. The question was of little importance except to the two countries concerned and, on a material basis, not even to them. But it was a warning that Wilson's idealistic principles were still far from being accepted by the peoples of Europe.

The great failure of the peacemakers was that their work stopped short in eastern Europe, at the frontiers of Soviet Russia. The armistice with Germany had annulled the treaty of Brest Litovsk. Nothing took its place. The victors could not make up their minds whether to negotiate with the Bolsheviks or to destroy them. In the end, they did neither. Wilson and Lloyd George proposed to invite the Bolsheviks and the various counter-revolutionary forces in Russia to a conference at Prinkipo, an island in the Sea of Marmora. The Bolsheviks agreed to come. The 'Whites' refused, and were supported by Clemenceau. The conference was never held. There was then a confused attempt at intervention, largely engineered by Winston Churchill. It achieved nothing except great expense and a permanent estrangement of the Bolsheviks from the rest of the world. The Conference devised a reasonable ethnic frontier between Russia and Poland, known as the Curzon line.

209. Japanese and Americans parade in Vladivostok

The Poles rejected it, and ended in 1921 by seizing much territory beyond it – to their subsequent undoing. Soviet Russia, exhausted by civil war and then by famine, was driven to accept most of the frontiers imposed upon her by the treaty of Brest Litovsk. She remained an outcast, her existence not acknowledged. Great Britain, France, Italy, and most European countries theoretically 'recognized' Soviet Russia in 1924. The United States held out until 1933, Czechoslovakia oddly until 1936. In a deeper sense, the non-Communist world has not 'recognized' Soviet Russia to the present day. This was the most important legacy of 1919. Lenin had aspired from the first to create a rival system of world politics. The statesmen of the existing world, instead of trying to win Soviet Russia back, did Lenin's work for him and pushed her further into isolation. When Soviet Russia returned as a Great Power, there was no place for her. Two Worlds had come into existence. Hence all our troubles at the present day.

Apart from this, what effects did the First World War have on the destinies of man? Contemporaries saw only the tremendous destruction, and were weighed down by it. The death roll reached an unprecedented total. France and Germany each lost a million and a half men – a graver loss for France

210. Lenin parades in Moscow.

211, 212. Death and famine in Russia.

with her smaller population. The British Empire lost nearly a million; Great Britain alone three-quarters of a million. Russia probably lost more than all the rest put together. American losses were slight – only 88,000. Add to these the greater millions of those crippled by the war, and the losses seemed staggering. Yet they left no permanent scar. No nation was permanently knocked out of the ranks of the Great Powers by these wartime losses, though France came near to being. Young males could be more easily spared than at any other time in the world's history, brutal as this sounds.

The material destruction was even more temporary. Though this, too, horrified contemporaries, it was on a comparatively small scale. On a map of Europe, the areas of destruction appear as tiny black spots: north-eastern France, parts of Poland and Serbia, a remote corner of Italy. Against this, though less noticed, were the new industrial resources which the war had called into existence. All the destruction was put right within a relatively few years, so that it was soon hard to find the evidence that there had ever been a great war. Most countries surpassed their pre-war production by 1925. Even Soviet Russia reached the level of 1913 again by 1927. At the end of the war, farsighted men, such as the economist J. M. Keynes,

213. A railway station on the Somme at the end of the war.

thought that the great problem of the future would be general poverty: they imagined that productive powers had been permanently reduced. Instead, within ten years, over-production became the great problem of mankind. The war, far from weakening economic resources, stimulated them too much. The most serious blow inflicted by the war economically was to men's minds, not to their productive powers. The old order of financial stability was shaken, never to be restored. Depreciated currencies, reparations, war debts, were the great shadows of the inter-war period – all imaginary things, divorced from the realities of mine and factory. Even so, the European standard of life was higher than it had ever been before.

In 1919, men expected social upheaval as well as economic disaster. They feared that 'Bolshevism' would sweep across Europe. Some few hoped it. Fears and hopes were alike belied. There was a short-lived Soviet Republic in Hungary, one even shorter-lived in Bavaria. Otherwise Bolshevism stopped at the frontiers of Soviet Russia. Private property and the capitalist system survived. The great aristocrats of eastern Europe lost their estates, usually after compensation; even so, those in Poland, Hungary, and eastern Germany escaped. The changes remained strictly political, and on a limited scale. Before the

214, 215. Victory parade in London, 1919.

216. Social unrest in France, 1921.

217, 218. General Strike in London, 1926.

war there had been only one republic in Europe, France; or counting Switzerland and Portugal after 1908, three. After the war there were more republics than monarchies in Europe. Before the war there had been four empires in Europe; after it, there was none. The Habsburg Monarchy broke up into national states; the core of the Ottoman Empire emerged as national Turkey; Russia and Germany survived somewhat diminished, but not Empires at any rate in name. The King of England was the only remaining Emperor in the world, in his capacity as Emperor of India; even that title had only another generation to run. All this seemed to show the triumph of democracy. Within a few years, many of these democracies became dictatorships. Men often blamed this on the war. Perhaps unjustly. The prestige of the old governing classes had long been decaying. When they vanished, dictatorships were as likely as democracy to take their place. War, at most, accelerated what was happening in any case.

The First World War turned essentially on the question of Germany. The Allies fought to restrain her; the Germans to win a political domination proportionate to their economic power. The war did nothing to solve the German 'problem'. On the contrary, its outcome made this problem more difficult than ever. Germany remained united, proud, still with all the resources of a Great Power. The restrictions on her were bound to prove temporary, unless the victors of 1919 enforced them by new exertions. Moreover, the balance of power had shifted in Germany's favour. Before the war, she was one European Great Power among five; now she was one among three, and clearly ahead of the others. Maybe, Austria-Hungary had been a German satellite, not a check upon her. But Russia had provided a balance in the east, reinforcing France in the west. Now Russia had disappeared as a factor in respectable politics. Italy hardly counted. France was left to balance Germany all alone. Things might have been different if the two Anglo-Saxon countries had continued in peace the stand which they had made in war. This did not happen. The British, having fought one great war, were determined not to fight another. Their only interest was to reconcile Germany and France, which meant in practice concessions to Germany at France's expense. The Americans went further. They repudiated Wilson's work and withdrew again into isolation. When new difficulties arose, their only contribution was to criticize others without doing anything themselves.

Immediately after the war, these practical difficulties seemed irrelevant. Though the peacemakers failed to solve the German question, some of them, particularly Wilson, believed that they had solved a greater problem: the problem of war itself. The League of Nations was expected to save the world from war in the future. The League received a great blow at the outset when the Americans refused to join it, perhaps however not such a great blow as was later alleged. British policy at Geneva, and still more the policy of the British Dominions, suggests that the addition of another Anglo-Saxon Power would not have been much help in making the League an effective instrument against aggression. The members of the League ran into two great difficulties as the years went by. First, the problem: what was the right course for peace – to defend the existing settlement or to revise it? Should the statesmen be firm or conciliatory? Should they choose resistance or appeasement? They chose each in turn, apparently at the wrong time. The second difficulty cut even deeper. The League existed to secure peace. How could this aim be achieved by going to war? Men had been told that, after the First World War, there would never be another. Later they were told that they must be ready to fight again so that this promise could be kept. 'Collective

security' was the slogan of the thirties. Another version of the same could be called 'perpetual war for the sake of perpetual peace'. The League, like other international systems, provided a tolerable machinery by which the Powers could conduct their peaceful relations, so long as they wished to remain peaceful. No more could be expected of it in a world of sovereign states.

The First World War failed to produce Utopia, resembling in this every human endeavour since the beginning of time. On a more prosaic level, it did rather better than most wars, though no doubt the price was excessive. The subjects of the Habsburg Empire obtained their national freedom; some of the subjects of the Ottoman Empire started on the same path. The war postponed the domination of Europe by Germany, or perhaps prevented it. The most practical war aim was the one most completely achieved. Belgium was liberated. The Belgians were the only people who fought the war for motives of un-alloyed heroism, from their king downwards; and they deserved that fate should vindicate them.

In all countries, the majority served and suffered for un-selfish causes which they did not fully understand. They all wanted a better world, though many of them wanted advan-tages for their own country as well. Ludendorff called the

British soldiers 'lions led by donkeys'. This character was not confined to the British, or to soldiers. All the peoples were in the same boat. The war was beyond the capacity of generals and statesmen alike. Clemenceau said: 'War is too serious a matter to be left to generals.' Experience also showed that it was too serious a matter to be left to statesmen.

221. Ideals put into practice: first meeting of the League of Nations Council, 1920.

Index

References in italics refer to plates and maps.